wtf?!
Why Teens Fail
What To Fix

Adam Brooks, Shannon Butler, Tanya Corder, Frank Griffitts, John Iannarelli, Laurie Latham, Katey McPherson, Brooke Scritchfield, Stephanie Siete, & Travis Webb

DEDICATION

We would like to dedicate this work first and foremost to our own families, who have supported us, pushed us, and believed in us. We hope that the advice we offer herein is never in vain and is put to good use in our own homes, with our own parents, spouses, and children wherever applicable. We dedicate this book to all other noble souls employed in the protection and educating of children, be they parents, guardians, public safety officers, educators, or counselors. May God bless you all.

CONTENTS

ACKNOWLEDGMENTS

BE THE ONE is a concept that evolved from Katey McPherson's SHE (Sharing Healthy Experiences), a forum of workshops for tween and teen girls to overcome relational aggression. SHE evolved into an event to provide leadership workshops for boys and girls and strategies for parents. We received overwhelming feedback from event attendees stating they desired more information than our workshop presenters were able to provide in the allotted times. Our presenters all agreed that they had much more information than they were able to convey during the workshops. Subsequently, BE THE ONE became the name of the company that produced this book and the team responsible for making the BE THE ONE events possible.

As the project manager for this book, I would like to thank each author for sharing their expertise and insights with us. I would like to thank their spouses and families for allowing them time to contribute to this work. I would like to thank the editing team at Creatsespace.com for their professional eye and substantial copyediting. Credit needs to be given to Amy Lytle for her photography and to Michael Hunter and his team at Entourage Marketing for the book cover design. And finally, we would like to thank all of the dedicated parents in the world who put their children's needs above their own personal interests in the hopes of raising up a new generation of happy and responsible adults.

A word about the title of this book. Like most children, it was produced through the passionate meeting of its parents. Unlike most children, however, this book has ten parents. The title was embroiled in controversy from the get-go. Some of us thought the double entendre was too suggestive for our more conservative audience members. Some of us thought the word "fail" portrayed us as unsympathetic or overly harsh toward teens in crisis. Indeed, with such sensitive topics as date rape and sexual abuse lacing our pages, our very last desire is to be so inhumane as to suggest that such victims are "failures." On the contrary, most of us subscribe to schools of thought that emphasize the positive over the negative. So why then such a negative title? At one point, we considered the substantially tamer title *What Teens Face* (yawn). However, being an eclectic mix of professionals with some disdain for political correctness, we felt best to call a spade a spade where applicable. We emphasize that the victims of violent crimes are NOT failures, but the acts themselves are, in the vernacular of our youth, "epic fails." They are failures on the part of the perpetrators and, in many cases, of society as a whole. And so, as responsible members of this society, we chose not to recklessly point out a problem without providing solutions. Thus, in addition to the edgy, slap-in-the-face *Why Teens Fail*, we propose a tertiary acronym for WTF: *What To Fix*.

--Frank Griffitts
WTF Project Manager

BE THE ONE

CHAPTER 1
THE NET -GENERS
BY ADAM BROOKS, HIGH SCHOOL TEACHER

I walked into my classroom this past year and told my new high school students, "This year we are concentrating on reading, so you all have to bring a reading book to class. If we aren't working on something, I want you reading!" I drilled into them the importance of vocabulary and how *leaders are readers*. But the next day when I asked them to read, I found that there were only a few books on the desks. This confused me because of our introduction to the importance of reading the day before. I was about to express my disappointment when I realized what was happening. Instead of books sitting out on their desks, there was an assortment of different types of reading technology: smartphones, electronic readers, and iPads, containing each student's selection of books that they wanted to read.

This took me by surprise because the school where I teach is in a lower economic bracket, and yet these students still had expensive devices and were using them to read. I realized right then that there was at least one major difference between this generation and past generations: these kids have access to advanced technology like no other generation in the history of mankind. I had always thought I was connected to this new generation. I was humbled to come to the realization that I was not as cool as I thought. I mean, I had a *pager* in high school. Students now have things like e-readers as standard operating equipment.

Why Teens Fail...

Teens have access to and mastery of technology beyond their capacity to understand the pitfalls that go along with the advantages of that technology.

What To Fix...

Ask your teens to teach you about their digital media gadgetry. Don't be offended when they roll their eyes at your lack of techno-savvy. Download their favorite apps. Play their games.

WTF

Young people born during the technology boom of the 1980s and 1990s are considered the Net-Geners (as in InterNET GENERation). Some even place Generation X and Generation Y in this group because they were the first students to have their woodshop and home economics classes replaced by computer literacy programs. It is easy to distinguish the Net Geners, though, because typically they have something attached to their heads—a cell phone or ear buds that allow them to listen to music on the mobile device of their choice. A recurring complaint I hear from parents in the previous generation is that their kids are constantly occupied by technology. Parents often feel that their own students have checked out of the "real" world and would rather participate with society over the Internet than in person.

Five Observations about Net-Geners

Parents, allow me to poke a little fun at you. At the risk of seeming judgmental, I am often amused at the irony when parents buy all of this technology for their teens without first understanding its implications. All I'm saying is that if we are going to pass judgment on the youth for seeming to be "not present," we adults ought to assume some responsibility for understanding the ins and outs of the technology we are all too ready to put into the hands of our kids. More on that in later chapters. But just as important as understanding the technology itself is understanding the technology-based social norms that comprise the world of the Net-Geners. Net-Geners generally...

1. ...are incredibly impatient and want things to happen immediately.
2. ...want everything catered to them.
3. ...are more socially conscious than any previous generation.
4. ...appreciate authenticity and what seems to be real over what is polished and seems to be fake.

5. ...have a tough time with social skills in the traditional sense and thus have redefined their social norms to include online or technology-facilitated relationships.

When parents take a look at these norms, they can begin to understand the thinking behind the decisions these Net-Geners make. The vices available to kids haven't changed all that much over the years, but accessibility has. For the most part the drugs are still the same; the weapons are still the same; the major issues around the world are generally still the same. The major difference now is that the flow of information has increased exponentially, providing instant access to information for both good and evil. If I wanted to do drugs growing up, I had to find those one or two kids at my school who were rumored to do drugs. Then I had to get up the nerve to actually talk to them face-to-face and solicit a deal. Now, thanks to the Internet, finding out what other students are up to is just a Google/Bing/Yahoo!/YouTube search or Facebook/Twitter/Instagram status update away. A quick IM (instant message) later, kids can have anything they want from anyone, all from the phone in their hand. With the prevalence of the smartphone, they can get any information they want at lightning speed.

It's no wonder that students of the current generation are more socially conscious then those of the past. With so much information at their fingertips, being informed about what is happening around the world is just a click away. When I was growing up in the 1980s, the only way I could find out about what was happening in the world was to grab a newspaper or watch the evening news. The Internet was around but still in its infancy, confined to the domains of the military and advanced educational institutions. This generation expects everything to be catered toward them because so many products offer them just that: the ability to customize their iPhones, their blogs, and social networking sites. With this new standard of technology, it is no wonder that they expect their environment to cater to them as opposed to adapting their own behavior and thought process to their environment.

Family-Talk Fridays

I have worked in the education field for many years, and a few years ago I was asked to teach a public speaking class. Since this was my undergraduate major, I was excited and readily agreed to take on the opportunity. I noticed, however, that as I talked to the class about how to communicate with each other and how the speeches would be presented, my students began to exhibit some anxiety. It is common knowledge that public speaking is a fear second only to death for many people. The students kept worrying about being judged by their peers if they messed up on their speech. So I attempted a different strategy. Rather than having them stand in front of each other formally, we sat in a circle and discussed their fears and insecurities. It became abundantly clear to me that I had unleashed a beast, so to speak. Our little discussion circle evolved into Family-Talk Fridays. Every Friday we began by sitting in a circle and someone would discuss an issue they were having with a friend or family member. As a class we would all brainstorm things the person could do to try to solve the issue in a peaceful and healthy manner. What I realized was that the kids in this generation want to know the how's and why's behind every decision an adult makes. If there is a new rule at school, they want to know why it was implemented. But what they really want is for someone to spend time listening to their thoughts. With only minor explanations from me, they understood and were more likely to follow the rules in question.

It dawned on me that we ask high school students to grow up, but we still make them stand in lines and expect them to do what they are told without question, much like elementary school kids. But these conflicting messages confuse them, and the more they are asked to "fall in line," the more they want to be heard.

What my public-speaking students wanted more than anything was to be heard and to get a glimpse of what was happening behind the scenes before they committed to the change. We discussed questions like, "Mr. Brooks,

---

Why Teens Fail...

"The young always have the same problem—how to rebel and conform at the same time. They have now solved this by defying their parents and copying one another."
—Quentin Crisp

What To Fix...

As parents, we lecture way too much. Another strategy: listen to your teen's problems and then ask them to tell you some solutions. Try not to rescue them from all their consequences right away.

why won't my mom let me go to a party on Saturday when she knows that I am a good kid?" We took the opportunity to talk through what could be some factors behind the parent's decision. This class occurred two years ago and I still have students come up to me and ask questions, wondering why they can't take my class again or why there aren't more classes like it on campus. Especially now that our economy is in such turmoil, schools don't have the time or resources to dedicate to the intangible skill of critical thinking, and parents are too busy trying to keep their finances, jobs, and families afloat. The students are left to question and wonder and worry and internalize everything they see and feel.

Why Teens Fail...

Critical-thinking skills are not being taught to our youth today. There are few places for them to go to gain these basic social skills and learn basic decision-making processes.

WTF

Without responsive adult mentorship, teens are forced to turn to their peers and the Internet for answers. If you think a teen's in-group can lead them astray, try a little Internet research on common adolescent concerns like, "Should I sleep with my boyfriend?" or "Is smoking weed really that bad for you?" This can be the beginning of destructive decisions for most teens.

As adults, we have learned how to separate what is going on in our lives and detach ourselves from reality if we need to. For example, if a couple is going through a divorce, they sometimes have the ability to endure the emotional turmoil and still be somewhat productive at work or in other facets of their lives because they have learned how to compartmentalize their emotions. Unfortunately, teens are not wired that way, because they have not yet learned the social and emotional skills needed to separate one emotional situation from another. If parents are going through emotionally tumultuous times such as divorce, it can devastate teens because they lack the life experience to compartmentalize their emotions.

Using divorce as an example, at the end of the ordeal the teen may feel like they have just gone through a divorce of their own—from their parents. This trauma seems to intensify their feelings of needing to grow up. Because they have the overwhelming desire for independence, they feel they are prepared to make grown-up decisions. They are making decisions about social

What To Fix...

Share your successes and your failures with your teens. They already know you're not perfect, so it's a good time to explain how some of your decisions led to difficult consequences for you.

13

drinking, casual drug use, sex, sexuality, or other decisions that come with risky consequences. If a relationship of honesty and open discussion hasn't been fostered between teens and parents (and sometimes even if it has), teens will turn to their peers or the Internet for advice. Never before in the modern age have students been so bombarded with messages from all around them that they need to grow up. But the messages detailing exactly how to do that are mixed to say the least.

Becoming a responsible adult is something that must be learned and taught to younger generations. Otherwise the unhealthy habits teens learn will lead them to become unhealthy adults.

Why Teens Fail...

Think back on some of the risky business you participated in as a youth. Now look at today's pop culture. Marijuana, for example, is practically legal and probably easier to obtain than alcohol or tobacco.

What To Fix...

Don't send mixed messages to your kids. The "do as I say, not as I do" mantra of our parents will not work with kids in today's world. Establish your family values and convey them to your kids.

Sara's Story

One of my students, Sara, found how something simple can become confusing. I gave students in my gifted reading class for honors students an assignment to pick a problem in society and research it to find possible solutions. Some students chose education. Another picked post-traumatic stress disorder. Sara chose teen pregnancy. She mentioned that a number of her friends had become pregnant at young ages and she saw the hardships that had occurred in their lives, so she wanted to attempt to find a solution. As she researched more and more, she saw statistics on teens getting pregnant in affluent neighborhoods versus those getting pregnant in lower-income neighborhoods. She also stumbled across statistics on teen pregnancies with regard to race. One day she came to me and said, "I think I know what would help solve teen pregnancy."

Her expression was one of shock. I said, "What's that?"

"Teens should sit down and talk about dating and relationships with their parents, and their parents should get more involved in their lives and ask questions about being sexually active."

"Wow, that sounds great!" I said.

"But Mister Brooks, this can't happen! The only thing I've ever heard my parents say about sex is that I better not get pregnant."

"Well, why can't this happen?"

"Because it's something that no one wants to talk about, especially not with your parents! Eeewww! Gross, Mister Brooks!"

Sara did more than just try and solve a part of teen pregnancy that day; she hit on a key factor on why teens are making unhealthy decisions: parent interaction. As adults, we find it easier to ignore a situation or avoid confrontation due to one of two reasons: (1) we are distracted by other factors going on in our lives; or (2) we may just be overwhelmed about where to start. But here is the key point of all my rambling:

Letting your teen make mistakes is a painful but crucial part of helping them grow up. Your teen needs a direct line of communication with you so that you can explain their options and consequences. Then they need to make choices and learn from their mistakes.

Teens need and deserve our undivided attention as they attempt to navigate the confusing messages they receive from their peers, other adults, and the media.

Teens are notoriously short-sighted. Scientists tell us that it is not really their fault, due to a general lack of frontal cortex brain development. But we adults don't have any excuse for being short-sighted. We must realize that the actions we take (or in this case, the actions we fail to take) may have serious consequences for our kids.

Why Teens Fail...

Teen pregnancy is only one of the major issues plaguing teens today. Sexting, dating violence, and drug culture are additional problems, to name only a few.

What To Fix...

Studies show that parents' talking to their teens has some of the greatest impact on their decision-making process.

Andy's Story

One of my favorite students, Andy, came to me his junior year with a serious issue. I say he is one of my favorites because there are many similarities between the two of us, and I understand his struggle. Andy has severe ADHD and constantly speaks before he thinks (for which I worked with him to improve his communication and social skills). We developed such a rapport that I could just shoot him a look and he would realize what he said that may have been rude or inappropriate and apologize immediately. I was never diagnosed with ADHD myself, but at times I do tend to speak without thinking, so connecting with Andy on a personal level was easy for me.

Andy's parents were separating and he came to me to talk through it. I told him the separation wasn't his fault and that his parents needed to figure out what was best for them as a married couple. Andy was seventeen at the time and very bright. He understood in his head what I was explaining, but he was having a hard time allowing it to fully sink in to his heart.

His mom came to meet with me the following week and I brought up the conversation I'd had with Andy. She asked me, "How can I let him know that this is between his dad and me and has nothing to do with him?"

I explained to her what her son had confided to me. "Andy is feeling everything that you and your husband are feeling because it is lingering in the house and he knows what is going on. He has a really big heart and so he feels emotions really intensely for his age. You can include him in going through this as a family or you can pretend like it isn't happening and leave him to figure it out for himself, but you have to choose."

This was an emotional meeting and there were tears. Divorce is not a light issue. But it is only one of many difficult issues that kids face these days. Times like these are when we have to stand up as the adult in their lives and help them navigate through these situations and emotions. It is at this juncture that they are most vulnerable. But they are often more teachable at those times, too. If we do not intervene and assist, someone else will. And that someone could be the wrong type of influence.

Why Teens Fail...

As parents, we often fail to demonstrate constructive conflict resolution in front of our kids, resorting instead to yelling and criticizing. The behavior we model will be internalized by our teens.

What To Fix...

Few people if any have "perfect" relationships. Practice modeling constructive conflict resolution in front of your teen. Afterword, involve your teen in a family debriefing to allay their concerns.

WTF

Eating Disorders, Body Image, and Spiritual Image

I have spent the last eight and a half years working at an eating disorder/anxiety health clinic in Wickenburg, Arizona. I work as their chapel speaker and I talk to the patients about how spiritual healing fits into the whole process. Without spiritual healing, the recovery process is much more difficult, if not impossible. I explain that we are multifaceted, holistic human beings, so we have to deal with life in a holistic way. I generally speak to two separate groups (girls ages seven to seventeen, and women eighteen and up). I still feel moved every time I look into the patients' eyes. I see their struggles as they open up their hearts. On some small level, I can relate to each of them.

Obviously, I am not a female and I have never had an eating disorder, but my connection with the patients goes much deeper. I grew up hating the skin I was in and had this intense desire to change myself so that I could be the way everyone expected me to be. Many of us can relate to that, including the patients I worked with in Wickenburg. These types of feelings typically start in the preteen and teen years. This insecurity will intensify if there happens to be any kind of abuse in their lives. If this type of thinking goes unchecked, it can lead the developing teen to unhealthy habits.

During my years at the clinic, I saw patients who came in with unhealthy eating habits that had escalated out of control. Many of these girls and women had been severely sexually or physically abused. Because of their inability to control the abuse in their pasts, many sought to control what they put into their mouths instead. Their stories were heartbreaking.

I had the opportunity to help these ladies rebuild their lives. Just hearing how some of them had been date raped, or molested by a family member, or beaten regularly by a significant other would be painful for anyone to hear, let alone experience firsthand.

WTF

> **Why Teens Fail...**
>
> *Many teens struggle because either they or their parents have some unresolved trauma in their lives (see Chapter 9).*

> **What To Fix...**
>
> *Be honest with yourself. Do you have unresolved trauma? Find out about available resources to help start the healing process in your life. Only then will you be able to help your teen when he or she is in crisis.*

But amazing things happen in the clinic, things that are held sacred by patients and staff alike. At the clinic, these women were forced to face what had haunted them for so long. In that clinical setting, many of them had their first opportunity to open up and share the skeletons lurking in their closets. It was rarely comfortable and oftentimes painful, but by talking and dealing with what had happened to them, they each found a voice that was never there before. And with that voice they began to conquer what had locked them away for so long.

I learned a valuable lesson from these resilient ladies: *Avoidance never solves anything.* The only way to become healthy is to face the past and move forward by practicing healthy decisions. One of these decisions is to

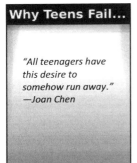

Why Teens Fail...

"All teenagers have this desire to somehow run away."
—Joan Chen

What To Fix...

"Feelings of worth can flourish only in an atmosphere where individual differences are appreciated, mistakes are tolerated, communication is open, and rules are flexible—the kind of atmosphere that is found in a nurturing family."
—Virginia Satir

get help by talking about trauma with a qualified coach, counselor, or doctor.

These young ladies and women were no longer silenced by their own struggles, because their struggles were no longer just their own. They no longer had to face the world pretending all was well on the outside with so much pain on the inside. The pain from their trauma did not go away all at once, but sharing their dark secrets within the appropriate setting became the first step on the road to recovery. It was along that difficult road of confronting the past and making plans for the future that they were again able to find their inner beauty and self-worth. Like these women, many of our teens are faced with similar trauma every day. As their parents and teachers, we must sometimes help our teens take the first step onto that hard road to recovering from trauma in their pasts.

The vision of this book is to help you think about the hard things that preteens and teens deal with every day and equip you with tools to start tackling some of the hard questions and situations that we face in our society. You may find some of the information in this book a little overwhelming. Lest I leave you in total despair, let me leave you with Cedric's story for a refreshing perspective.

Cedric's Story

About six years ago I had a very bad accident on the freeway. I rolled my car going seventy-five miles per hour, and I wasn't wearing my seatbelt. As I climbed out of the car, I realized that everything had been thrown from the vehicle except me. I found my glasses a few feet from the wreck. I looked around and saw my CDs scattered across all lanes of traffic, mercilessly crushed under passing tires. Someone was looking out for me, though, because when my car had finally landed on the roof, a metal post had gone through my windshield and lightly scratched me in the back of the head. But other than that, I had sustained no other injuries. After the accident I made a decision. If life was this fragile, I wanted to do every job I thought would be fun and to travel to all the places I'd always wanted to see. So I took a job as a pizza delivery guy, because who doesn't love pizza? Then I took a job as a barista, being around drinks I loved. I'm not gonna lie— the caffeine was enjoyable! But the one thing I had always wanted to be was a camp counselor. At this point in my career I had been teaching for several years and my summers were free. I looked up camps and became overwhelmed by the number of options available. I selected one that was appealing and sent in my application.

Texas Lions Camp, which served students with physical disabilities as well as various other medical conditions, called me for an interview. A week or so later they offered me a position for the summer as a camp counselor during their ten-week program. I was nervous as I flew out to Texas, but stepping off the plane put me into a world that would last a lifetime in my heart. The entire goal of the camp was to make sure that any camper, regardless of their disability, felt as though they belonged and that they were "normal" (though, as we all know, no one is actually "normal"). The campers who attended our summer program had a variety of disabilities, everything from traumatic brain injury to asthma. The campers' needs varied according to their conditions. I had to learn sign language because a few of the campers were deaf; others were missing limbs or had cerebral palsy, which required more assistance or other accommodations. The main goal for the camp was to assist campers with achieving their personal goals while they were there for the summer. Whatever they dreamed of doing, we would assist them with turning it into reality.

Why Teens Fail...

"Just after I entered my teens I suddenly entertained an insatiable enthusiasm for the delightful habit of criticizing others."
—Loretta Young

What To Fix...

"It is time for parents to teach young people early on that in diversity there is beauty and there is strength."
— Maya Angelou

For example, one of the activities we engaged in was helping wheelchair-bound campers to climb a rock-climbing wall. This was accomplished by placing the campers in a harness and hoisting them up. Several camp counselors would hold the weight of the campers' bodies while the campers used only their hands to climb.

Another example was a camper I met who was born without arms. This kid learned to shoot a bow and arrow with his feet! Being a counselor at that camp was an incredible experience that has found a special place in my heart.

During my second week at camp I met a young man named Cedric. He had asthma and had never been to camp before. Cedric was a heavyset boy who weighed close to three hundred pounds. All the guys in the bunkhouse fell in love with Cedric right away because he had a smile so big that his eyes would close when he was happy.

One night we took all the boys camping outdoors. I was sitting at the dinner table with Cedric, discussing how he was enjoying camp so far. He looked at me with his big eyes and said, "Well, it's my first time away from home, so it's fun but I miss home. I haven't left the house much in the last few months."

"Oh really? Why is that?"

"Well, a few months ago my mom was sick and me and my dad went to go get her medicine and when we came back she had passed away. I've been wanting to put up a picture of her under the bunk, but do you think the boys would make fun of me?"

My heart broke for him and I said, "If they do I will end them, Cedric! You put up whatever you want. I think that is awesome and your mom would love that!"

After a few moments of silence I asked him, "Cedric, what is one of the things you would love to do while you are here at camp?"

"I want to climb the rock wall!" he said confidently.

This made my heart skip a beat. We had lifted campers bound in wheelchairs before, but considering Cedric's weight, I wasn't sure if we would be able to help him up the wall and toward his goal. Immediately I began attempting to politely discourage Cedric. I was worried that we would not be able to make his one dream come true. I told him that we would try our best, but maybe there were some other events we could do that might be better, like maybe doing archery or going swimming. He would not be budged.

The next day, as we were all walking toward the rock wall, I began to worry because of what I thought was sure to come. They had tied some harnesses together for Cedric, gotten him a helmet, and prepared him for his adventure. He came over, grabbed my hand, and said, "Come on, Adam, watch me!" I followed him to the base of the rock wall and he ensured I had a front-row view. I began to pray for a miracle to help Cedric complete the rock wall course. He approached the wall with confidence and put his foot on one rock, grabbed another with his hand, and stepped his other foot up, steadying himself. He took one more step up and then he fell down.

My heart fell into my stomach. My mind was racing. How was I going to be able to console him, and how would I be able to spin this defeat into something he could be excited about? Then Cedric turned around, and I will never forget his face. He wore the biggest smile I had seen from him the entire summer of camp. He came over to me and said "Adam, Adam, did you see that? Did you see how far I got? I went farther than I have ever gone in my life!" He was ecstatic! Then he asked, "Do you think my mom would be proud of me?"

That's when the tears hit and a lump came to my throat. I looked into his eyes and said the only thing anyone could. "Of course your mom's proud of you! I'm sure your dad's proud of you! I'm proud of you! I think the grass is proud of you!"

There is so much we can learn from Cedric's story. I learned that it is so easy to look at our lives and see only how far we have left to go and to realize that we are not where we want to be in life. We want to have a better job or have more stuff. Our teens want to be more popular or just graduate and finally start a career or college. What we rarely do is look back at our lives and see how far we have come. Cedric knew what I did not, which is that it is important to realize that we can choose to come farther along each day and to never be scared of potential failure.

> **Why Teens Fail...**
>
> *Teens are afraid of what other people think of them, and this drive to conform can put them in a bad or difficult situation with friends.*

> **What To Fix...**
>
> *Share what is on your mind so teens don't have to assume what you are thinking. Have family dinners once a week where each person can share uninterrupted for two minutes about what's been going on in their lives.*

Every one of us will fall off the rock wall of life from time to time. We just have to have the courage to get back on and take the next steps.

As parents, we might not ever completely understand what's going on inside the heads of our teens, but we can have the courage to begin to discover a new relationship with them that will be healthier than it was yesterday. We don't have to worry about overcoming our challenges; we just have to worry about taking the first few steps and knowing that we can be proud of them.

CHAPTER 2

IF THE WALLS COULD TALK...
BY KATEY MCPHERSON, SCHOOL ADMINISTRATOR

Old-School Bullying

Many parents hear the word "bully" or "bullying" and picture a big kid on the playground towering over someone smaller. Or perhaps images of taunting in the boys' locker room come to mind, where swirlies and de-pantsings still happen. But times have changed, and the word "bullying" has come to be known as "relational aggression," "harassment," or "intimidation." I am sure as you read this, your experiences as a child are flooding back into your mind as you recall the events that marred your "perfect" school life. There is a quote that says, "Many people won't necessarily remember what you said, but they will remember how you made them feel." Ain't that the truth!?

When I was in school, my "bullies" were girls, and they were *mean*. I met one of the biggest bullies I've ever known on the first day of seventh grade, sitting in homeroom. Because her name followed mine alphabetically, I was destined to have her in my life every day for the next six years, sitting in front of her and sharing a locker, all the way through my senior year in high school. I will never forget the day, very early on in junior high, when she turned around and looked at me, high as a kite, and said, "I am going to kick your ass." For the life of me I had no idea what that meant, nor what I had done, but I was scared to death!

Another time, I was trick-or-treating with my childhood friend, Cindy, and the meanest, biggest bully in our school came up and stole ALL of our candy. She ran by us both, grabbed our pillowcases and just kept running. I was devastated. It was awful. I cried myself to sleep that night. She was so scary I didn't want to go to school the next day for fear she would taunt me. That happened twenty-eight years ago and I can still tell you who I was with, where I was standing, and how I felt. Proof that those memories never leave us!

I went home and told my mom I'd accidentally left my candy at Cindy's house—and she believed me! What child leaves her candy at a friend's house on Halloween night? (Newsflash and Parent Tip 101: If your kid's story sounds weird, something is up, investigate!)

Many of you probably have similar stories of unfortunate events or people who came in and out of your adolescence. Most of us came out alright, apparently unscathed but still scarred. I can still to this day tell you what I was wearing and doing when another mean girl approached me and told me that because I was dating her ex-boyfriend (which at that time meant talking on the telephone and listening to heavy breathing when you did talk, not even really seeing each other at school), she was going to meet me under the bleachers at the next high school game and show me what "not so pretty" looked like. Again, I was scared to death!

These scenarios play themselves out and certainly happen every day in our schools. For the more resilient kids, these become character-building experiences that help them navigate hostile territories throughout their lives. For others, these same experiences can be devastating roadblocks to future happiness. We have to teach kids how to self-advocate and how to report.

Why Teens Fail...

Bullying has always been around and it likely always will be. In the age of digital media communication, there are increasingly new ways for bullies to commit their acts of aggression.

What To Fix...

Become familiar with your school's policies and procedures. Most schools have a Code of Conduct manual that parents and students must sign at the beginning of the school year.

WTF

A Few Statistics to Consider

I live in Phoenix, Arizona, and a few years ago, the Dove Corporation did a survey of teen girls' self-esteem and their connections with their parents. Among their findings:

Two-thirds of girls (67 percent) in Phoenix believe they are not good enough or do not measure up in some way, including their looks, performance in school, and relationships with friends and family members.

The majority of teen girls (65 percent) reported engaging in negative activities, such as disordered eating, cutting, bullying, smoking, or drinking, when feeling badly about themselves:

Fifty-one percent of teen girls admit to talking badly about themselves. Thirteen percent resort to injuring themselves on purpose or cutting when feeling badly about themselves

Thirty-one percent practice disordered eating, such as starving themselves, refusing to eat, or overeating and throwing up, when feeling badly about themselves

The self-esteem tipping point happens during the transition to teenage years, resulting in a loss of trust and communication with adults:

Sixty-seven percent of girls ages 13–17 turn to their mother as a resource when feeling badly about themselves, compared to 89 percent of girls ages 8–12.

Only 32 percent of girls in Phoenix ages 13–17 will turn to their father for help when feeling badly about themselves, compared to the 47 percent of girls ages 8–12. At 16, girls become more likely to seek support from male peers than from their own dads.

Parents' words and actions play a pivotal role fostering positive self-esteem in teens:

The top wish among girls in Phoenix is for their parents to communicate better with them, which includes more frequent and more open conversations, as well as discussions about what is happening in their own lives.

Why Teens Fail...

In general, 5 to 10 percent of kids frequently use relational aggression as a means to manage their relationships. The other 90–95 percent watch those kids bully others every day.

What To Fix...

Parents and educators need to learn how to empower the bystanders to take action when bullying is observed to intervene in a positive and healthy manner.

WTF

In general, 5 to 10 percent of kids frequently use relational aggression as a means to manage their relationships. The other 90–95 percent watch those kids bully others every day. It happens in the locker room, on the bus, in the bathroom, on the field, via text messages, on Facebook, and within their music and TV viewing.

Kids these days have taken the world of meanness and relational aggression to a whole new level—but not on their own terms or by their own doing, by any means. Every day when I am done with work, I look at my colleagues and say, "It is not their fault." Many factors play a role in the explicit use of meanness, disrespect, and outright exclusion that goes on each and every minute in our schools. Some of these factors are blatant, others not so much.

Relational Aggression: A Learned Behavior

Our Net-Geners and Millenials bully in all sorts of new ways. They use nasty text messages, eye rolls, exclusionary glances, "un-invites" at the lunch table from their favorite friend, or "de-friending" or blocking on Facebook. None of this is much different from when I was in school, these are just new tools at kids' disposal to advance the hurt. It travels faster than we can speak.

Primarily, as we know, mass media, marketing, and TV reality shows are not doing any favors for our societal moral compass. Shows like *American Idol* and *16 and Pregnant* not only inundate our families with harmful messages, they are teaching our children that it is okay to make fun of people. Mixed messages abound as we American families sit around our living rooms and make fun of the people on these shows, the models, actors, and singers together—and the worse the performers are, the "better" the evening, and the "better" our conversations at work and school are as we exchange juicy information about the latest scoop of meanness.

Our kids sit in the backseat as we slam the other parking lot moms at the schoolyard, degrade our spouses on the phone to our friends, and light up the latest

---

Why Teens Fail...

Our kids listen to everything we do and say. Do you cuss out other drivers with your kids in earshot? Have you ever degraded your spouse or another adult in front of your kids?

What To Fix...

To the extent that we are able to use constructive vocabulary around our children, they will model that behavior when they have problems with their peers.

neighborhood gossip. Without realizing it, we are modeling the mean-spirited behavior we want our kids to stop and of which they are frequently the victims. We are teaching them that it is okay to put another person out of our circle of caring and refer to them as an "it." We need to make progress on the road to civility and humanity or we are in big trouble. One of my favorite authors, Larry Winget, author of *Your Kids Are Your Own Fault*, says that we should think of our children as thirty-year-olds and work backward. What do we want them to be like, look like, and act like? How do we hope they will represent us? And more importantly, how should they treat others? As fantastically horrible as reality shows are, they are abundant with relational aggression and contain key ingredients to set our children up for failure as we launch them into the real world.

According to Nikki Brown, author of *Girl Fighting*, relational aggression is defined as "behavior that is purposefully harmful to one's relationship with others." Examples of relational aggression include gossiping, teasing, taunting, eye rolling, exclusion, and hurtful comments about one another.

In America in general, most of our students come to school each day excited about something, whether it is friends, food, or a teacher. They are by and large equipped and ready to learn at some level. I am not referring to their academic progress, but rather to their social and emotional growth, and the feeling they get when they think of themselves in relation to others, understanding perhaps that "I am a community member of this school, and I matter to someone."

> **Why Teens Fail...**
>
> *The pressure to fit in and be popular is immeasurable in middle school. Peer approval is just as important or more important to most kids than their parents' approval.*

> **What To Fix...**
>
> *Parents can balance this out by spending time with their kids to build self-confidence and self-worth. Too much criticism is the one thing that pushes kids away from Mom and Dad more than anything else.*

I can determine within the first five minutes of the school day how much learning is going to go on based on how students enter our school door. If they are greeted by their friends, it is going to be a great day. If they are not invited to the next party or a seat at the same table as their friends, academic work can forget it—brain shutdown is on the horizon.

Now you are probably disagreeing with me, thinking you packed them a great lunch, bought them the new t-shirt they wanted, or filled their backpack with new school supplies. Your home influence does of course play a huge part on your children's attitudes and lives, but more than anything, their social group has the ability to trump any decision you make for them.

Middle school and adolescence, as we all know, are times for students to navigate socially turbulent waters. They are filled with tumultuous emotions riddled with arguments, ridicule, pressure, and a constant changing of costumes as they parade around school looking for that recognition and welcome as a member of something bigger than themselves. They attach themselves to anyone and everyone they can relate to, listen to music that supports their beliefs, and insert themselves into causes that further their aspirations. Slowly but surely they form a vision for themselves as to what they would like their path to look like. As a parent, you have to have faith that your child will invite you to be a part of this. The only way to insure it is to BE PRESENT, SUPERVISE VIGILANTLY, and LISTEN INTENTLY alongside them.

Why Teens Fail...

Widespread anecdotal observations suggest that most kids really start to develop independence from their parents around age twelve. This can lead to some bizarre behavior.

What To Fix...

Don't take it personally when your teen disagrees with everything you say just for the sake of disagreeing. Patiently but firmly stand your ground on the important issues.

Tween-agers and Social Development

What does relational aggression look and sound like? Well, that depends. My research and focus is on fifth to eighth grade students and how they transition from being tweens to teens, so I focus on that group here.

If you were to visit a fourth or fifth grade classroom, which is typically full of nine- and ten-year-old girls and boys, you would see and hear them say things like, "Let's play the invisible game and pretend she is not here" and "Look at his clothes, they are so gay."

If you were to visit a typical sixth grade classroom, typically kids aged eleven and twelve, you would see and hear things like, "I am so over her. She is always talking behind my back and spreading rumors. I heard she stuffs her bra anyway." Typically this is the age where sexting also begins. Requests from boys for pictures of "nudes" are often granted, with no reciprocation wanted or given.

Raw data as well as discipline data shows that in seventh grade, teenagers start to engage in more experimental and risky behaviors, and that relationally aggressive behaviors skyrocket. Many kids move through stages and certainly they will test the waters as they are reaching, stretching, and growing as individuals. I receive many phone calls to my office each week from distraught parents asking if their child has been taken over by demons, or if there is possibly something wrong with them. They are desperate to find the answer and are willing to pay whatever it takes to fix it. The answer is simple: there is no "fix," and the work is the family's to bear. You are raising a tiny adult who is growing at the speed of light, whose prefrontal cortex has not formed quite yet, and whose body is growing faster than they can sneeze.

The phone calls I receive often start with, "I don't know what happened to my son or daughter, but they are not doing their homework, they have constant excuses for me, and they lie right to my face."

"Yup," I say. "And?"

Walking the Tightrope

This Dr. Jekyll/Mr. Hyde behavior is pretty typical for teenagers, and when handled correctly it can be a fantastic learning experience for kids and parents as well. As parents, we tend to make one of two mistakes: we push too hard, or more dangerously, we give up too easily, afraid that our children will fail. No pressure here, but it is our responsibility as parents to find the balance and walk that fine line between those two extremes. No pressure...*right!*

Not one of us wants to believe that our child is a failure. So to be fair to the child, a failing child is more often than not a reflection of failed parenting. Our sole purpose on this earth as parents is to protect our children, shape them, mold them, and guide them.

> **Why Teens Fail...**
>
> *Parents sometimes overcompensate for their teens "failures" and try to rescue them from every consequence.*

> **What To Fix...**
>
> *Remember that most failures are not permanent and generally make the best learning experiences. Allow your teen to take a few healthy risks and then face the consequences of their decisions.*

As parents, we have been charged with a tremendous task of raising our children and guiding them through each phase of their lives. There is no going, back and giving up is obviously not an option.

So, if your children are failing, or if you have failings as a parent, take heart: very few, if any, failures are permanent. In fact, some of the world's greatest success stories arise from the ashes of failure. We learn our greatest lessons from defeat, and if we persist, we may turn our worst failures into our greatest successes!

Watching students from a school standpoint, navigating the seas of social competence is a lot like watching your children learn to walk and eat solid food. You know, when you shovel the rice cereal into their mouths and they basically puke it back up all over themselves and you? Did you then force feed your child more than she could eat? Did you stop feeding her altogether? Of course not. You instinctively found the balance and made sure she had just enough to eat.

When your child was a toddler, did she fall down a lot and scrape her little knees as she was learning to walk? Was it possible for you to catch her every time to prevent the owie? Of course not. But hopefully you were there 99 percent of the time to pick her up and brush her off. You gave her boo-boos a kiss and wiped away her tears and set her back on her feet.

Just as you found the balance between letting your little one take a few bumps and keeping her safe, so too can you find the balance between letting your teen have a few minor failures on her own without swooping in and saving her from the consequences of her actions. Raising a teenager is a process, and sometimes you have to let them fall before they can get back up, but you cannot let them do it alone.

But just because your seventh grader acts like a miniature adult and thinks she knows everything doesn't mean she has all of the resources yet to overcome every obstacle or adversary that crosses her path, or even do something as simple as organizing a backpack. You still have to know when to let her stumble and when to keep her from running out into a busy street without looking both ways!

Why Teens Fail...

"When your teenager wants you the least is when they need you the most."
—Larry Winget

What To Fix...

We may need to rescue our kids from time to time, but the best way to do so is to provide them unconditional love and emotional support as they face the consequences of their actions.

WTF

Unnecessary Failure Opportunities

Time and again, I have seen parents and school administrators inadvertently set their children up for unnecessary failures by allowing them into dangerous situations or scenarios that are prime breeding grounds for relational aggression. Such breeding grounds give way to nightmares and landmines for parents and schools to undo. Here are a few danger zones of which to be extremely wary:

see p. 33

1) Sleepovers. Nothing good happens at a sleepover! I repeat, NOTHING GOOD HAPPENS AT A SLEEPOVER!
2) Twin/Spirit Days. There is nothing good about trifectas and girls. Three is never a good number, and Twin Day always sets up someone to be left out.
3) Band trips and rooming assignments. Allowing kids to choose their own room assignments just leads to someone being excluded (again). When in doubt, assign rooms randomly or pick straws. Allowing kids to handle this will only lead to trouble.
4) Field trips and "buddies."
5) Birthday parties. Invite everyone or no one
6) Water park excursions. Bikinis and Daisy Dukes: body image issues and teasing and taunting abound.
7) School Dances

> **Why Teens Fail...**
>
> *There is no way for all kids to be included all the time.*
>
> *Cliques will always be a part of teen life.*
>
> *There is often no way to avoid hurt feelings from these scenarios.*

Am I suggesting that our tweens should never be allowed to engage in these seven scenarios? With the exception of the maybe the sleepover (I have seen too many horrific incidents as a result of a sleepover), most of these situations are more or less inevitable. But with a little coaching preloaded on the front end, most of the drama can be mitigated.

> **What To Fix...**
>
> *Parents can help their kids understand that everyone gets left out sometimes. We can also encourage them to be inclusive rather than exclusive when it's their turn to decide who gets to come.*

WTF

Fostering a respectful home environment is one of the key ingredients a family (of any shape or size, married, widowed, or divorced) can provide a child. Handling conflict is not easy in any family, much less one that is a housing a teen or tween. Their struggle for autonomy coupled with your quest to make them responsible, law-abiding citizens, is charged so full of ups and downs it can be likened to a pregnant woman on steroids.

School Administrators and Asylum Wardens

When people ask me what I do for a living and I say, "I work at a middle school," they usually gasp and tell me that I must be crazy, out of my mind, or brave.

I agree with them! It takes a special person to watch the agony these kids go through, the lashing out that goes on, and the real-life dramas that make soap operas look like Girl Scout meetings. I admit that part of me thrives on the challenge of redirecting their awkwardness, takes pride in coaching them through difficult decisions, and then marvels as they forget what I've taught them before the next time they have to take a pee. I've heard it said that the definition of insanity is doing the same thing over and over again and expecting different results. Middle school is like an insane asylum in so many ways. Here are a few anecdotal accounts to help you see middle school through the eyes of a school administrator.

Two Balls, One Wheel

I have many stories that would make you laugh until it hurts. One such fond memory is of a student reporting to me that he had a "wardrobe malfunction" with his shorts and that the button had popped off. I asked him if he had a change of clothes and he said, "No, but it wouldn't matter anyway. I forgot to wear underwear today...I'm going commando." As I unlocked the bike gate for him to get his bike to go home and change, I noticed it was 104 degrees out and he was mounting a unicycle!

WTF

Psssssst...Hey, Kid, Wanna Buy an iPod?

A few years ago, a student decided that he would tell fellow students of his school bus that his dad owned

---

Why Teens Fail...

Some kids have a special knack for painting a big flashing neon sign over their own heads that says, "I'm an easy target, pick on me!" Developing their social skills and social competence is not easy, but it is possible.

What To Fix...

We've all put ourselves in awkward situations before. Some of us excel at it. We can counteract this classic attention-seeking behavior by giving our kids lots of positive attention at the right times.

Best Buy. He promised he would bring each student an iPod to school in the next few days if they each gave him ten dollars. Sure enough, kids pulled out wads of money and invested in Mr. Best Buy, Jr.

And sure enough, his Dad had nothing to do with Best Buy (he was actually an accountant for an insurance firm!). Every day the boy boarded the bus after his proposal, the crowd of kids who had invested grew angrier. He eventually came clean on the bus, threw a wad of money in the air, and screamed, " Here you go!"

Some students who had not invested of course grabbed money, and those who actually had were left empty-handed and with ten dollars less to their names. The impulsivity of the teen brain is fascinating, and the inability to see Antecedent + Behavior = Consequence is perplexing, yet understandable to those who explore this topic.

Nothing Good Happens at a Sleepover

I repeat (ad nauseam), nothing good happens at a sleepover. One Monday morning I was greeted by a group of young ladies, nervously giggling and hiding their cell phones. GUILTY was written all over their faces and I questioned their movement. They replied with the standard teen response—"nothing"—and moved on. Later that day, they resurfaced in my office, bewildered and frightened. I invited them in and once again, they were giggling. It was apparent they were embarrassed. Wearing my oh-so-subtle counseling hat, I asked what was going on. It seemed there had been a sleepover, and one of the activities entailed taking "nudes," as they call them and sending them (which is called "sexting") to their male friends. In return, the male friends were supposed to send them photos of their own private parts. Well, the boys started first, and the girls decided that they shouldn't return the favor and instead "accidentally" sent the text to the entire contact list on their phones. Yep, this is the story I call "The Penis That Went Around the World in Thirty Seconds." Again, nothing good happens at a sleepover!

WTF

Why Teens Fail...

Sending nude photos, or "sexting," as it is more commonly called, is only the tip of the iceberg when it comes to sleepovers.

What To Fix...

You will hear this again, but it is a really good idea to have a digital media contract with your kids, outlining expectations for behavior when using online media, including their phones.

The Importance of Communicating

I realize there is an entire chapter toward the end of this book related to communicating with your teen, but I have to take a couple of sentences to underscore the importance of communicating as it relates to relational aggression. Students who experience bullying behaviors or RA will not always come forward and report their experiences. Often if they have a few friends, they will confide in one or two. Students in my office will always say to me "I wish my parents understood" or "I wish they would honestly just *listen* to me." As a parent of four daughters myself, I often jump into the Mama Bear mode and try to fix it too soon, before I have all of the information. I have learned that sometimes you just have to "wear it around" and let the process play out.

In order to best help your child, and to raise a socially competent individual, the following conditions should be present in your home:

You're Not the Judge of Me

Teenagers are judged all day long. You might as well liken it to lights, camera, action. They are judged by themselves in the mirror (which they look into all day long if they are female), in the halls, in the locker room, in the bathroom, at the lunch table, in their classrooms, by their siblings, by their clothes, by you, by their relatives, by their peers...the list goes on. This is why they come home and fall apart! They sass, they rant, they say mean things to their siblings, they are unappreciative...you name it, they are often like a ticking time bomb emotionally. Let them be themselves and embrace them. We are all living on borrowed time. Make theirs count.

WTF

What NOT to Do or Say

This is one of the most difficult positions for a parent to be in. What do you do? What do you say? Most parents I have gotten to work with do a great job raising their children. I work in an area where students come to us

---

Why Teens Fail...

Parents often assume that they know exactly what their kids are going through and begin communication with statements like, "When I was your age..."

What To Fix...

Make it a point to check in with your tween two or three times a week. Ask about which friends they're hanging with. Ask them who made them happiest or angriest today. Follow up with "Why is that?"

well equipped, ready to learn, and most truly excel and live the life their parents dreamed of their having. However, as the economy has tumbled and times have changed, we have seen a tremendous amount of stress on kids, and I believe that most are living in crisis.

Marital strife and divorce, job loss, foreclosures, parental drug use and other addictive behaviors…the list goes on, and it is literally destroying families. No one has remained untouched by the damaging effects of the economy and its losses, and those who rode it to the hilt, leveraging all of their savings and equity, are paying a dear price. More and more kids are bearing the burden of responsibility for household chores and jobs, and are needing more and more attention. The problem is that more parents are not able to give it due to their newfound economic hardships.

Modeling appropriate communication and conflict resolution strategies will go a long way when your child encounters a less-than-favorable situation at school—and they will be see, hear, and feel *many* personally. One of my favorite authors, Rosalind Wiseman, outlines a fabulous tool for creating social justice champions in our schools. In my opinion, every child who exits high school should know how to:

Maintain their dignity

Be socially competent

Be media literate and technologically savvy

Why Teens Fail...

Teens get talked AT and told what to do all day long. The older they get, the more they resent being told how to manage every aspect of their lives.

The Controlled Failure

You *want* your child to have fantastically horrible experiences—under your roof. You want the experiences that make them stretch, think, and grow, and even if they make you grow gray hair, you still want it to happen under your guidance and supervision, as opposed to in the police station! In order for that to happen, you have to give them a little room to flex their wings and try to fly on their own.

What To Fix...

Start by offering your tween a few limited options. As they get older, make them tell you what their options are. Coach them accordingly. Talk about the natural consequences of those options.

They may fall out of the nest a few times and get a few bumps and bruises, but when they're ready to soar for the first time, they won't be surprised by the crosswinds that will surely buffet them along the way.

How do you shape this model of a child who fluidly moves from group to group, who can self-advocate and stand up for and to others, and who is cognizant of their surroundings and how respect is shown and given?

The Trifecta: Bully, Target, and Bystander

The three players in any bullying incident are (1) the target or victim, (2) the bully, and (3) the bystanders.

In days of yore, the schools would focus on the bully by giving him a swat with a paddle in the principal's office. But those days have been long gone for decades. I think it is safe to say that no kid in the public school system has gotten a swat with a paddle (or any form of corporal punishment, for that matter) for thirty years or more.

In more recent times, I used to worry mostly about the targets of bullying. We spend a lot of our resource dollars and professional development trainings talking about what to do for kids who are bullied. As the pendulum has swung away from bully-oriented problem solving, we spend very few hours talking about the bullies themselves. Typically, we say things like "rough home life," "it is not their fault," "the apple doesn't fall from the tree," or "his brother was trouble." We make sweeping generalizations about why these kids might bully, but we have pretty much already given up on them before they even get out of the gate.

I have news for most parents: NO CHILD is unscathed by having a rough home life. Rough is relative to what all of our families are dealing with in this new world. Parents whose children are targets of the bully never just forget about the bully. They want justice! And when the school is incapable of dealing with a bully, the parents of the targeted children often turn to the campus police officer for a little old-school-style justice (see Chapter 3).

Why Teens Fail...

As a society, we have limited the public school system's ability to enforce discipline by relegating it to detention, suspension, diversion programs, or expulsion as a form of consequences.

What To Fix...

Parents must understand that most schools have specific behavior policies with a specific range of consequences. Also, privacy laws forbid administrators for disclosing which punishments were doled out.

WTF

The Bystander Solution

As an educational community, we have finally figured out that we have overlooked a facet of the bully equation that may hold the answer to the problem: the bystander. We have finally begun to empower children to stand up for each other and denounce the unjust acts they witness by their peers.

One in four situations could be avoided if bystanders would become what the movie *Bully* calls "upstanders." These upstanders rarely report what they see. Out of 950 students at my school, it is what my principal would call the 5 percent rule. Five percent of kids will engage in relational aggression, five percent will engage in risky behaviors, 10 percent will talk like they are involved in it when they really aren't, and 95 percent will watch it happen.

If you are a parent of our 95 percenters, what do you want your children to do if they saw someone being bullied? Who do you want them to go to? Do they have a "safe" person both at home or in your extended family and at school whom they can go to? Have you ever sat down and told them that no matter what they tell you, it will remain confidential? You (and your spouse, and extended family) are the protective factor in their lives—act like it! Ask questions about their day; don't get too nosy, but probe to keep a pulse on what is going on in their daily grind. When in doubt, carpool. You don't even have to say a word to learn everything you want to know about your teen and their friends. It is like word vomit—they get in the car and it just keeps spewing!

Here are three real-life scenarios. I would like you to process what you would expect from your child if she were faced with these uncomfortable situations.

Your sixth grader is undressing for PE. The girl next to her is eleven and is wearing a blinged-out thong that says "Can't Touch This." She starts making fun of your daughter's "granny panties."

> **Why Teens Fail...**
>
> *Parents and students are often unfamiliar with their school's incident-reporting policy and therefore fail to take advantage of the procedures provided. Schools cannot fix what they do not know about.*

> **What To Fix...**
>
> *Know your school's incident-reporting policies. Understand that investigations take time.*
> *Understand that some situations may get worse before they get better as all parties are educated in the process.*

Your child overhears eighth graders in the bathroom stall talking about blow jobs. She doesn't even know what that means.

A boy in your child's science class is seen rolling something up in papers and sticking it underneath his sock.

If you have a campus that has outlined expectations for students as to how to report these behaviors, you will have no problem directing your child for help. Most schools have mandatory reporting forms from the school district driven by the state as well as their own internal incident report forms.

Students need to be taught that they have dignity and no one has the right to take that away from them. They need to know that their voice should be heard and no one has the right to silence it.

An Impromptu Interview

Today as I was writing my book, I saw the cutest boys sitting at the table next to me at the Paradise Bakery Café. I asked them if I could interview them and they said, "Sure!"

"Does your school have a bullying program?" I asked.

"Uh…," they said.

"You know, to stop bullying," I prompted them.

"Uh, I guess," said one boy. He looked to his friend for support, trying to figure out why this strange lady was talking to them.

"Yeah," said another. "We do."

"Good, " I said. "What is it called?"

"I dunno," came the expected response. "There are just stickers and stuff everywhere that say BULLY with a line through them."

"How do you report bullying?" I asked. Blank stares.

Why Teens Fail…

Parents are often angry and feel inclined to blame the school for lack of protection. This is understandable but sometimes leads to unproductive communication between parents and administrators.

What To Fix…

Schools require specificity. Dates. Times. Locations. All parties involved. How it started. How many times it occurred. All subsequent communication between involved parties.

"What about your teachers, do they help you when you get in a sticky situation on the playground or with a friend?"

" No, my teacher just likes to text and read emails while we have free time so she isn't very helpful."

"Okay. You guys have been really helpful," I said with what I hoped was a kind smile.

This chapter is not a bullying program. If it is, it explains exactly why "bullying programs" don't really work. On that note, I have fourteen "bullying programs" on my shelf in my office. These are things we have adopted over the last fifteen years of my career. Not one has lasted more than a year. Thousands, probably hundreds of thousands of dollars have been wasted on this district-wide.

If you have any further questions about exactly what constitutes bullying in your area, ask your school principal for a copy of the district's student code of conduct handbook. The book describes exactly what constitutes a policy violation and often outlines possible consequences. Remember, school administrators will not be able to disclose specific punishments or consequences given to specific students. Neither will they relate any consequences for your student to another parent or student. That would be a violation of the student's privacy under FERPA (Federal Equal Rights Protection Act) and most school district's policies.

How Does This Whole Book Apply to Bullying?

<u>Net-Geners (Chapter 1)</u>
Remember that teens of this generation are extremely connected socially via digital technology. Technology is a double-edged sword. In the history of mankind, the amount of information available to our students today is unsurpassed. But they also have a zillion new ways to torment each other. Running pass interference on the Internet is not easy.

<u>Digital Downfalls (Chapters 3, 4, and 5)</u>
Cyberbullying? All over the place! Phone sexting? It's an epidemic. Webcam sexual harassment? It's all the rage!

Phishing and identity theft scams? Kids can be victims too. Know the dangers and talk to your kids candidly about social responsibility and their digital reputations.

Safety (Chapters 6, 7, and 8)
Partying is what college kids do, right? Yes, but it is starting younger and younger all the time. Do you know what the drug of choice is these days? Does your teen understand how risky behavior can lead to a slew of dangerous situations, including sexual assault?

Trauma and Communication (Chapters 9 and 10)
This book is about bullying and other related dangers. Take time to learn about trauma, how it may have affected you, and how it may be affecting your child. Learn ways to correct the devastating effects of trauma and communicate in a healthy manner with your teen.

Enjoy the rest of this book!

Works Cited

Winget, Larry. *Your Kids Are Your Own Fault. ; The Principles for Creating Responsible, Productive Adults.*. New York: Gotham Books, 2009.

Wiseman, Rosalind. *Queen bees & wannabes: helping your daughter survive cliques, gossip, boyfriends, and other realities of adolescence.* New York: Crown Publishers, 2002.

CHAPTER 3
FOUR PITFALLS OF THE INTERNET
BY FRANK GRIFFITTS, POLICE DETECTIVE

I am a husband, a father of seven great kids, and a police detective working in the computer crimes unit of my police department. I have been doing cyber investigations in one form or another since about 2004. In my experience, there are four major pitfalls that parents and teens need to be aware of when it comes to cyber safety and potential dangers on the Internet. These areas are:

(1) Fraud
(2) Cyberbullying
(3) Extreme/mature content
(4) Sexual predation

Allow me to share a few professional experiences that underscore the importance of safeguarding yourself against these dangers.

The Shoe Princess Walks Down Easy Street

I learned from dealing with other people's goofy kids what I did *not* want my kids to turn out like. As my hair gets a little grayer (read: more distinguished) I sometimes say "kids," but what I really mean are young adults who have failed to grow up. I was born in the early '70s and from my generation on, I think we are all guilty to some degree or another of this one thing: we all grew up thinking the world owed us something and that life should be as easy for us now as it was when we were kids. Because we weren't yet born or were too young to remember, we forget that our parents had to sacrifice and work hard for their success stories. We were somehow, myself included, under the false impression that success would come to us because we deserved it. Most of us have finally figured out by now what a load of crap that is.

Don't get me wrong, I'm all for positive thinking and law of attraction stuff. But somewhere along the way, many of our parents failed to teach us good old-fashioned work ethic and goal-setting skills. Now, I am really grateful to my parents for the good values they instilled in me, but I want to make sure that my kids don't grow up thinking that the world owes them anything—for the obvious reason that it simply does not. My thoughts turn almost immediately to the Case of the Shoe Princess.

I was working as a financial crimes detective when I got an investigation of a twenty-something female passing bad checks at a couple of hotels and a shoe store at the mall. When I finally tracked down the Shoe Princess, I found her renting a room in a little bungalow near downtown Phoenix in a little bit rougher part of town. I put her in handcuffs, read her her Miranda Rights, and asked her why she was trying to cash bogus checks in my town. (No, I'm not the sheriff, but it sounds a lot tougher when you say things like "my town.") This was her story: The Shoe Princess explained that she had quit her job and was out of money and in need of a roof over her head. In such a desperate situation, she looked on the Internet for a job and found what she thought looked like a perfect work-from-home employment opportunity. I should point out that many a college student has fallen prey to this online scam.

Why Teens Fail...

College kids have it rough. Remember back in the day? So much stress. You had homework, and... and, uh...social life, and...uh....Let's be honest, if you saw a work-from-home job, you'd have been tempted too!

What To Fix...

Anytime you are asked to move money from point A to point B and then back to point A again... DON'T. This is likely some form of money laundering. And point B (you) always gets stuck in the middle.

WTF

Apparently, textile manufacturers in the United Kingdom have some difficulty in cashing travelers' checks in the UK, so they hire "accounting assistants" in the United States to help them process their funds. The Shoe Princess thought it was totally legitimate to work as an "accounting assistant" even though she had no background whatsoever in accounting, and soon received three thousand dollars in travelers' checks in the mail. The alleged employer emailed her instructions to deposit the money in her checking account, keep 10 percent for herself as wages, and forward the remaining 90 percent to her new employer back in the UK. There was one small problem: the Shoe Princess did not have a checking account, so no bank would cash the checks for her. The alleged employer then sent her emails threatening prosecution if she did not return their money (I guess they don't know how to stop payment on checks in the UK). And the Shoe Princess, without so much as a background in basic, high school consumer mathematics, claimed that she didn't see anything fishy with their bogus story either.

Now desperate for food and shelter, the Shoe Princess decided to use the travelers' checks to lodge at a couple of different hotels, all the while supposedly under the assumption that the checks were from a legitimate company. At some point, the Shoe Princess had to have known the checks were bogus, because she bounced from hotel to hotel to avoid being caught for bouncing the checks. Way too much bouncing in that last sentence, but I digress.

Here is my favorite part. When she finally realized she was in over her head and needed Daddy (a wealthy manufacturer of designer shoes) to bail her out, she went to the department store and attempted to buy a pair of designer shoes (her father's brand) with the bogus checks, because she could not dare to show up at her father's house to ask for help in a pair of ratty old gym shoes.

Why Teens Fail...

I don't know if she was telling the truth about her wealthy daddy, but her behavior was indicative of a kid whose daddy bailed her out of trouble every time she made a bad choice.

What To Fix...

Try letting your children suffer natural consequences for the bad choices they make when they are younger. It is much easier than letting them suffer when they are older and the consequences might involve jail.

Now, the Shoe Princess obviously must be held accountable for her own actions as a mentally competent adult (yes, the courts will find you mentally competent even if you don't take consumer mathematics in high school), but it happens to be my humble opinion that at least part of the blame here can be placed on poor parenting. Did Daddy somehow fail to convey to his daughter that his success does not come overnight without a great deal of work and sacrifice? Did he frequently bail his daughter out of predicaments throughout her life, thus enabling her to continue to make poor decisions well into adulthood? Did he fail to mention that few things worth doing are ever easy?

Xena the Cyberbully

"The story you are about to hear is true. Names have been changed to protect the innocent." My name is not Joe Friday, and (as is often the case in criminal investigations), even the victims are frequently not so innocent. Nevertheless, both the victim and the suspect in this case are thirteen-year-old girls, so their identities are protected under state law. The year was approximately 2004. MySpace had been around for about a year, but had not yet hit the scene in a big way. Mark Zuckerberg had launched Facebook about that same time, but it was still in its infancy. Even without these two major players dominating the social networking scene, kids were already discovering the thrill of social networking on various blog sites. I was a patrol officer in an upscale neighborhood, working the swing shift. I responded to my first call of the day straight from briefing right after 4 p.m.; some mother was frantic that her thirteen-year-old baby girl had received a death threat on the daughter's Internet blog profile. Mom and daughter met me at the front door and invited me in.

Mom explained that her daughter Blondie (not her real name) had held a slumber party the previous Friday night. A couple of girls, including Xena the Warrior Princess (not her real name), were there, and the girls decided to get on the family computers for some good old fashioned instant messaging. Blondie was upstairs and Xena was downstairs, and they were having a good time instant messaging between themselves and a certain boy on whom they both had a crush.

Why Teens Fail...

BFF (Best Friends Forever) is a title of honor. It takes a very long time to earn the coveted status of BFF with someone in middle school. This equates to about two weeks in middle school time.

What To Fix...

BFFs should NOT share locker combinations.

BFFs should NOT share Internet account passwords.

BFFs should NOT share crushes on the same boy. Duh...

The boy, as I understood it, was not at the slumber party, hence the need to be on both computers instant messaging each other simultaneously in a bizarre cyber love triangle. Not surprisingly, Blondie and Xena became jealous of each other and vied more desperately for the boy's attention as the night went on. By morning, Xena went home enraged that Blondie would say such horrible untruths about her to the object of their affections.

Naturally, when Blondie received an anonymous comment on her blog profile the next day that stated, "You are nothing but a f***ing Jew…you make me want to slice your f***ing throat," both Mom and Blondie were a little alarmed. (Yes, they were Jewish, and I suspect the nasty little anti-Semitic element might have exacerbated the problem.) While Blondie was pretty sure that Xena was not actually going to decapitate her (they had been BFFs* for like, OMG*, over two weeks), Mom was not convinced that Xena was harmless. I was not particularly thrilled with the prospect of doing a criminal investigation on a thirteen-year-old girl, but as an officer of the law, I had to give the investigation due diligence.

Mom presented me with the evidence by handing me a stack of papers that represented a printout of Blondie's blog profile with the alleged threat. Actually, it appeared that the printout was copied and pasted from the blog profile into a word-processing document and then printed. A side note about criminal investigations: while copied and pasted text is one form of evidence, the actual saved log file is far better and much more likely to be admitted into court than something that could easily have been altered by the accuser (a word-processing document, for example). Regardless, I looked at the printout and observed a couple of things. First, Blondie's profile screen name was—and I'm not kidding here—*iluvplayboybunnies69*. I read it aloud and looked at Blondie with the most condescending glare I could muster. "Really?" I asked. She blushed and looked away. I glanced over at Mom.

"We talked about that," Mom said with a reassuring nod.

"Great," I said. Mommy's little angel shifted in her seat and I imagined that she was readjusting her halo as she tucked a blonde lock of hair behind her ear. I read down the printout. In case you were wondering whether the words from the blog post (i.e., "you make me want to slice your f***ing throat") were meant as an actual threat, Xena followed up at the very end of her rant with the

Why Teens Fail...

Cyberbullies are sometimes under the false impression that Internet allows them to have completely "anonymous" relationships with acquaintances or strangers.

What To Fix...

Understand that there is no such thing as being completely anonymous. Understand that if a victim desires prosecution, police have no discretion and charges must be filed if there is evidence of a crime.

Why Teens Fail...

Having mingled with middle-school- and high-school-aged kids, I can attest firsthand that they have the filthiest mouths you will ever hear. And it gets worse on the Internet for some reason.

What To Fix...

Using the Internet should be considered a privilege rather than a right. Maybe as a precursor to your child using the Internet, you could have a discussion about your family's values and what behavior you expect.

incriminating statement, "and that's a f***ing threat!" It should also be noted at this point that these charming young ladies did not at any time use asterisks in their comments—I have censored the actual words with asterisks to protect your virtue, dear reader.

Based on my conversation with Mom and Blondie, the content of the comments made it quite clear that it was in fact Xena on the other side of the anonymous rant. Something I think parents and teens alike should come away with from this discussion is this: there are very few venues for pure anonymity on the Internet. With the right court orders (subpoenas or warrants) and enough political pressure, just about every IP address can be traced to its originating source computer.

Knowing this, but not really wanting to expend the energy to do all that paperwork, I contacted Xena and her parents by phone and explained that I knew it was Xena who had posted the anonymous comments on Blondie's blog profile. After a few lame attempts at denial, Xena finally admitted that she in fact made the comments "just to get Blondie to shut up." I explained that Blondie and her Mom were insistent on prosecution and that I was duty-bound to file misdemeanor charges against Xena at the local juvenile court. To make a long story short, she had to stand in front of a judge and try to explain herself. She lost and was slapped with a juvenile criminal record that probably did not look too good on any of her college or job applications throughout her teen years.

Be the One

In Chapter 2, Katey talked about the importance of teaching kids self-advocacy skills when it comes to relational aggression. Can you think of some ways that the Xena situation could have been mitigated?

Usually, in any bully situation there are three parties: the bully, the target, and the bystander. We try to teach our kids not to be bystanders. Rather, we would like them to become "upstanders." We teach them to Be the One. Be the One to stand for social justice.

What does that mean? Does that mean starting a fight with the bully in vigilante superhero fashion? Not at all. But how your child chooses to be an "upstander" is totally dependent on your child's personality. There are generally two types of "upstanders." First, there are the highly vocal, out-in-front-of-the-crowd leader types. They're not afraid of anyone and they have the charisma and social skills to control a situation without resorting to violence. They comprise a very small percentage of the population. If your child is this kind of leader, you already know it. If you don't know for sure, there's a good chance your child is like the other 99 percent of us.

The second group of "upstanders," the much larger group, are the behind-the-scenes leaders. They quietly go about their business, doing what is right because it is the right thing to do. They don't like to jump into the mix and create more drama. Most of us fall into this category. So which strategy works best for each group?

Type One Leaders: The Out-In-Front Leader

Type One leaders know who they are. They just have that confidence about them. They probably don't need much advice on how to intervene. They've already stood up and told the bully to knock it off. Or better yet, they took the bully aside later and said, "Dude, I like you, but I don't like the way you handled that situation with so-and-so." If the Type One leader needs any coaching at all, it might be to help them with a little bit of tact. Other than that, they already have the confidence and most of the skills to diffuse a situation. To these kids, I say, "Good job! Be the One!"

Type Two Leaders: The Behind-the-Scenes Leader

Type Two leaders are the good kids who know that if they try to intervene when they witness a bullying situation, one of two things is going to happen: either they are going to create more unwanted drama, or they are going to become a target for the bully themselves. So how can Type Two leaders Be the One? There are two strategies. First, they can try what the Type One leader did in the example above. If they know the bully and have a rapport with him/her, they can take the bully aside sometime and express empathy for the bully's target in such a way as to make the bully think about his/her behavior. If your Type Two leader isn't comfortable with that approach, there is actually something even more powerful they can do. Type Two leaders excel at finding the targets, putting an arm around their shoulders, and saying, "Hey, that bully is one of my friends, but I just wanted to you to know that I like you too, and I didn't really agree with how [the bully] handled that situation. I think you're an okay kid."

Obviously, my lingo is not kid lingo. They will have to say it in a way that is meaningful to their peers, so they don't sound like a forty-year-old cop. I can think of a couple of Type Two leaders who made a big impact on my life growing up and changed my self-image and self-confidence.

Be the One in Cyberspace

How can your kid Be the One on Facebook, Instagram or any other social media? It's easy. When your kid sees a bully harassing someone online, encourage him or her to send a text or a private instant message to the target to give them a little positive moral support. It doesn't have to be epic. It doesn't have to mention the bullying. It just has to counteract the negative influence of the bully. That small kind gesture might mean all the difference in the world to the target of the bullying that day.

Happy Birthday, Mr. Hitler

I agree that the title of this segment is not particularly politically correct. This is intentional for a number of reasons. One, political correctness is almost never funny, and with such somber subject matter, I feel compelled to try to keep it as light as possible. Two, anything that says "happy" and "Hitler" in the same sentence has to make you say "eww." Most people probably find such word combinations tacky, tasteless, or gross, but nevertheless morbidly compelling, like a bad traffic accident. Third, apart from the shameless gimmick to keep you, the reader, interested, the title actually does tie in with the subject of the following narrative.

The date, as I recall, was Thursday, April 19, 2007. I was a school resource officer on a campus that joined a middle school and a high school. My partner over at the high school was gone that day, so when a kid contacted the principal about other students possibly bringing weapons to school to do harm, I had the happy job of interviewing the student and taking the report. Up until that morning, I had been a little bit disappointed by the completely uncharacteristic lack of chaos at the schools that third week in April (please reread that last sentence with a sarcastic tone). The third week in April is traditionally one of the busiest weeks of the year for school administrators and school resource officers. It might have something to do with the date of April 20 being Hitler's birthday and a celebrated holiday for neo-Nazis and white supremacists. But more than likely, it has everything to do with kids being strung out and overdosing on massive quantities of sugar left behind a couple of weeks before by the Easter Bunny.

Why Teens Fail...

April 19th is the anniversary of the Waco siege in 1993 and the Oklahoma City bombing in 1995. April 20th is the anniversary of the Columbine High School massacre. 420 is also the police code for marijuana.

What To Fix...

Have your kids be vigilant all year long for peers acting crazy, but they should be especially observant in April. Better yet, tell your kids to be nice to everyone. Their kindness might prevent a tragedy someday.

Well, this one turned out to be the real deal. The reporting student, wishing to remain anonymous for her own safety, said she overheard some peers talking about stealing chemicals from the school science laboratory and setting off some explosions that were intended to "make Columbine High School look like Disneyland."

I decided to take her seriously for a couple of reasons. One, because as a cop, I am obligated to take things like that seriously, especially when the potential for bodily harm or death to a large number of students is even remotely possible. Two, I was aware of a current investigation involving just such a burglary from the school's science supply closet. Three, there had been another report of chemicals being used to start a fire at an elementary school over spring break. And finally, I was only behind about six reports, and they were a lot less

Why Teens Fail...

Hate propaganda websites can make a huge impression and have a severely negative impact on impressionable minds. Some websites can show you how to build explosives using household items.

What To Fix...

Supervise Internet use. Know what your kids are looking up on the Internet. Limit the hours your kids have access (computer bedtime).

interesting (like iPod thefts, disorderly conduct, and other boring stuff).

Since it was the 19th and the next day was the alleged target date of April 20, and potentially much more exciting than we wanted it to be, time was of the essence. We got the names of six teenage boys who were reportedly involved, rallied our resources, and that same evening knocked on all six of their front doors simultaneously. At the end of the day, all six boys were arrested for third-degree burglary with additional evidence that included a stockpile of ammonium nitrate (the same stuff Timothy McVeigh used to blow up the Federal Building in Oklahoma City on April 19, 1995). Detectives later found evidence on the boys' computers linking to websites espousing neo-Nazi ideologies and instructions on how to build explosives. Thankfully, we will never know if we narrowly averted a disaster of epic proportions, but it is a little disconcerting to think of all the horrific possibilities nevertheless.

The young man I spoke with that night appeared to be every bit the mainstream American teenager as you could imagine, complete with a more or less pleasant and articulate disposition, fashionable dress, and even a fairly conservative haircut. His mother kindly invited us into their upscale home in a relatively affluent neighborhood. Mom was genuinely concerned. The young man appeared to want to help us with whatever he could, denying all involvement in anything nefarious. At first. He admitted that he did not want us to look at any files or Internet history on his computer in his bedroom, but he insisted that it was just because he had some pornographic material on there that he was too embarrassed to let anyone see (though he reportedly had visited websites with extreme political views encouraging violence).

But my juvenile suspect's story began to unravel as his less savvy friends elsewhere started to cave under the pressure during their police interviews. While I was still at this young man's house, I received a couple of phone calls from my counterpart detectives, explaining that several of the other boys had admitted to doing the burglaries and that my suspect appeared to be the ringleader. When confronted with this accusation, he promptly invoked his Fifth Amendment rights and asked us to leave his house. We had to explain to Mom that we could not leave, because we now had probable cause to detain them and secure any potential evidence in their home until the judge signed the search warrant. It was a long night whose ordeal ended over a year later when at least four of the six boys indicted were charged with various felonies.

Why Teens Fail...

An unsupervised computer in the bedroom of a teenage boy will without fail have some form of pornography on it. And that may not be the worst of it.

WTF

Older Men Make Disgusting Lovers

As a school resource officer, I was the scary guy on campus. I came to work every day in full uniform, which included a utility belt with a badge and a gun, a tactical/bullet-proof vest complete with radio, extra handcuffs, and a Taser. I wasn't exactly the guy you would think kids would come to and divulge their deep dark secrets. That was why I was a little surprised one day when I was in my office typing up a report on a stolen iPod when a twelve-year-old girl knocked on my door and poked her head in my office.

What To Fix...

Keep computers out of kids' bedrooms. Know all of your kids' email accounts, social network accounts, and corresponding passwords. Sure, they deserve a little privacy... when they're out of YOUR house.

"Go away. I'm busy," I declared without looking away from my computer monitor.

"P-please, Officer Frank. I need to talk to you about something," the young girl sputtered with a nervous quiver in her voice.

Ungh. What now? I thought. Another stolen iPod, no doubt...

"Officer Frank, I did something stupid," she said.

"I'm shocked," I said, not trying to hide the sarcasm from my voice. "What did you do?" I asked dryly, doing my best to sound uninterested (which was actually pretty easy).

"I sent my boyfriend a picture from my cell phone," she sniffed.

I took a deep breath, not really comprehending what she was telling me. "What's wrong with that?" I asked, exhaling slowly and noticing for the first time that she appeared genuinely distraught. I don't know if it was the tears pooling on top of her lower eyelids

Why Teens Fail...

Almost all healthy teens (boys and girls) are sexually curious and eager to learn about the opposite sex. Technology has made it increasingly easy to explore sexual relationships without the face-to-face element.

What To Fix...

Talk to your kids about sex. These days, you probably want to start basic conversations about appropriate boy-girl relationships in grade school (kids are growing up faster and faster these days).

or the wide-eyed and distant stare in her face that told me something might actually be seriously wrong.

"It wasn't a picture of my face," she said.

"Oh." I tried to swallow the bad taste I'd just noticed in my mouth. "What was it a picture of?" I asked out loud before I realized I didn't really want to know the answer to that question.

The corners of her mouth curled involuntarily downward as her chin began vibrating violently and the tears breached the dam of her eyelashes. She came in and sat down with her face hidden in her hands, blubbering almost incoherently. The picture, I learned, was actually more than one picture. One was of her bare breasts. The other was a rather compromising close-up involving her index finger and her feminine orifice. I called for a school counselor to help me with the delicate issue of trying to salvage the young girl's decimated self-esteem and then proceeded to investigate the details of the incident.

In 2007 in Arizona, the state law did not differentiate between "sexting" (minors transmitting sexually explicit images of themselves to other minors) and adults transmitting sexually exploitative images of minors. I was facing the dilemma that was a common problem for law enforcement at that time in Arizona: according to state law, it was a felony to possess, send, or receive images of sexually exploited children, but common sense dictated that children should probably not be charged with a felony for behavior that most would consider to be morally objectionable, but few would consider to be criminal in nature.

To complicate matters further, I learned that the girl had never met the young man in a face-to-face meeting. She did not even really know who he was except that he sent her a picture of himself when he "asked her out" via text message. A mutual friend of theirs had given her phone number to him. He was supposedly fourteen years old and attending a middle school several miles away. Flattered by a little attention from a boy two years older than she, she agreed to be his cyber girlfriend. Then the predatory behavior commenced.

The young man began asking her to send him nude pictures. At first she resisted, feeling as most girls who have any self-respect would feel. But he persisted. She consulted her friends about what she should do. Much to my horror and disbelief, her friends reportedly told her something along the lines of, "It's just a picture. Everyone is doing it. Don't be such a prude."

Why Teens Fail...

Teens feel an enormous amount of pressure to fit in and feel desirable. All men are pigs. Okay, not all men are pigs, but they are hunters at heart. Hunters love trophies. A nude picture of a girlfriend is a trophy. Hunters show off trophies.

After continuous encouragement from her cyber boyfriend and her so-called friends, she succumbed to the peer pressure and sent the pictures. After she sent the first couple of pictures, she was ensnared. Now he was able to tell her to send more pictures or he would break up with her…and everyone knows what ex-boyfriends do with naked pictures of ex-girlfriends (hello, fame and glory on the Internet).

What To Fix...

Talk to your kids about sexting. They already know what it is, trust me. Tell your girls that once a picture is sent, there is no "un-send" button. A couple of minutes of indiscretion can ruin a kid's digital reputation for years to come.

To make a long story short, I called the principal of the young man's school and told him that there might be sexually exploitative images on this young man's phone. The principal spoke to the young man and searched his phone. They reportedly found no contraband images on the young man's phone. Deleted. Or worse…already uploaded to the Internet. Regrettably, there was no real evidence of criminal behavior and no way to take the alleged exploitative pictures back. This was the first of many similar incidents involving young girls, older boys, and cell phones that I would investigate over the next couple of years. That particular young girl learned a very painful lesson.

Now Can I Get On the Internet?

There are a handful of other colorful but true stories that I would have liked to have shared with you at this time, but regrettably, your attention span and the space allocated for this book do not permit (for more stories, see my blog at http://WTF-WithTheFuzz.com). I chose these four stories because I believe they aptly illustrate the key dangers of fraud, bullying, extreme content, and sexual predation. I could have told you the story about the kid who filled out the bogus online survey and gave away his parents' credit card information. Or I could have told you about the jerk kid who hijacked his friend's social network profile and made all kinds of inflammatory sexual orientation comments. Or I could have told you about all of the idiotic behavior kids learn about on YouTube and other video sites. And maybe I should have told you about the long list of sexual predators who have been caught trying to get very young girls in the sack with them. But I think I've already terrified you enough for one day.

To end this chapter on a positive note, I would like to share with you some ideas that can help you to facilitate your kids' safely navigating the Internet. Remember how I said at the beginning of this chapter that I have seven kids? They currently range in age from six to sixteen. Admittedly, the strategy that my wife and I employ would probably not work with my older kids if I were only just now starting to implement it. The secret of my success in keeping my kids safe on the Internet has been preparing them with safe Internet strategies since they were eleven or twelve years old. It started out something like this (and I paraphrase the conversation according to my best recollection):

My twelve-year-old son approached me one day and said, "Dad, all my friends have Facebook profiles. Can I have one?"

I said, "Facebook says you have to be thirteen to have an account with them, but let me talk to your mom." His mom and I discussed it and came to the conclusion that there was an immense amount of peer pressure to have a Facebook profile among young teens and that if we did not allow it in the near future, there was a good chance that he might be tempted to make one without our permission at a library or at a friend's house. Admittedly, this is a dangerously permissive attitude. Taken to extremes, I have seen parents rationalize underage drinking parties at their houses based on the same justification, saying, "It is better if they do it under my supervision." I vehemently disagree with this strategy when it comes to consuming alcohol or drugs due to the dangerous health ramifications as well as the legal liability associated with such risky behavior. However, in spite of my awareness of the vast array of Internet-related crimes, I was unable to see any parallel dangers with the Internet as they pertained to health or criminal liability.

After discussing these points with my wife, she said, "The Internet is a valuable tool and is probably not going to go away any time soon. Kids need it for homework and it is becoming a huge social medium. How do we instill the right values in our kids so that they make good choices on the Internet when we are not able to look over their shoulders anymore?"

I thought that was a valid point. We discussed the idea of using the privilege of the Internet to reinforce our family values. Years before, my wife and I had decided that we needed to have ten family values—ideas that were important to us as a family and that would give our kids a sense of identity. Our ten values went through a couple of iterations, but we finally settled on the following lineup:

FAITH, HOPE, CHARITY, LOVE, VIRTUE,
KNOWLEDGE, PATIENCE, HUMILITY,
DILIGENCE, and OBEDIENCE.

After this discussion with my wife, I went to my twelve-year-old son. "Son," I said, "you will be thirteen years old and in junior high in a few months. I will let you have a Facebook page on several conditions."

"Okay, Dad," he said with mild excitement.

"First, I want you to memorize our ten family values. Can you do that?" He nodded thoughtfully in reply. "Second, I want you to learn about each value and what it means to you personally and to you as a member of our family."

"Okay, Dad," he said with slightly less excitement, but a resolve to take on this responsibility none the less. When he asked again about Facebook, he was almost thirteen and we had several discussions in the following weeks about our family values. It was a great opportunity for me as a father to express my thoughts and philosophies about life in a way that directly applied to some of the things my kids were going through. It was probably the day after his thirteenth birthday that he was back and asking for permission to get on Facebook.

Why Teens Fail...

Your teen's notion of values like virtue are probably different than yours. Even with candid discussions and positive interference, your teen may exhibit behavior that you disapprove of once in a while.

What To Fix...

Help your teen see the consequences of their decisions. Coach them through difficult times with unconditional love. They may stumble and fall, but your love will help them find the right path.

"Son," I said, "these are my final conditions. You have to give me your email and your password to your Facebook account. You have to ask for permission to use the Internet every time you want to use it [our home computers only have one user account and one password that only my wife and I are privy to]. And lastly, you have to recite the family values and possibly even talk about one of them every time you want to log in."

"Wow, Dad. You're insane," the look on his face said. I smiled because deep down inside, I knew the look on his face was right. I am crazy. Love for my kids has done that to me. Well, that and the fact that there are seven of them and there is never a quiet moment in my house and their schedules are all over the place and they listen to crap music and they dominate the television and the video games and their friends are always over and... but I digress... again.

So that was the Internet tradition that my wife and I started. It is a little bit tedious to be the custodian of the Internet, but now all of my older kids have a Facebook account. Once every couple of days, they come up to me or my wife and ask, "Can I get on Facebook?" Then I just raise my eyebrows expectantly. They roll their eyes, sigh, and say, "Faith, Hope, Charity, Love, Virtue, Knowledge, Patience, Humility, Diligence, and Obedience. Now can I get on the Internet?"

"What's virtue?" I ask.

"Virtue is self-control. It means being pure and honest and kind."

"You're a really good kid," I say. "Are you going to exercise virtue while on Facebook?"

"Yes, Dad." Another long sigh. "Now can I get on the Internet?"

"Now you can get on the Internet."

PARENT RESOURCES

http://www.WTF-WithThe Fuzz.com

http://www.azag.gov/children_family/netsafety.html

http://www.netsmartz.org/internetsafety

FBI - in charge of cybercrime in AZ - He gave the lecture. I went to 5/11. Very good -

CHAPTER 4
YOUR CHILD'S IDENTITY (THEFT) CRISIS
BY JOHN G. IANNARELLI, SPECIAL AGENT

Your Child's Identity (Theft) Crisis

You have spent years trying to teach your children how to manage their money. You gave them an allowance and expected them to perform chores in order to appreciate the value of a dollar. Now your high school senior is getting ready to go off to college and is applying for financial aid and student loans. However, they find they are rejected due to a poor credit rating. How can this be?

Even kids who have never applied for credit in their lives can have bad credit, thanks to criminals who engage in identity theft.

Most of us are aware that identity theft is a significant problem, and that it's important to take measures to protect your identity from would-be thieves. What people might not know is their children can also be targets of identity theft before they even become old enough to own a credit card.

As if bad credit is not enough, what about your child's reputation? If someone steals their identity, will it prevent them from getting their first job? Even worse, what if they have a criminal record before they are even old enough to attend school?

The Federal Trade Commission has identified child identity theft as a growing problem and encourages parents to do what they can to minimize the risks to their

> ### Why Teens Fail...
>
> *In order to be a victim of identity theft, all you have to do is nothing at all. In other words, you have to take proactive steps to protect your identity and your financial security.*

> ### What To Fix...
>
> *As parents, you will need to check your children's credit scores periodically to make sure that someone has not tampered with their identities. More on this later.*

children. According to the FTC, more than 3.5 million kids have been affected, and that figure continues to increase, with the number of child victims of identity theft having increased by more than 30 percent over the past decade. The most common way a criminal can steal or misuse the identity of a child is to get the child's Social Security number. Generally, parents apply for an SSN when their children are born, but then they tend to forget about it. Because of this, identity theft of a child's SSN can take years before it is detected, which creates serious consequences when that child comes of age. Identity theft could affect your child's future credit and employment history if the thieves obtain credit card accounts or get jobs using your child's identity.

Criminals use the SSN to open credit card accounts, obtain loans, rent an apartment, sign up for utilities, get cell phone service, or even apply for a job. Credit issuers often do not have a way to verify the age of the credit applicant, so the criminal only needs to change the age of the identity associated with your child's Social Security number, providing the necessary information for the approver so that the criminal can receive fraudulent credit.

Once the first fraudulent account has been established in your child's name, it becomes even easier for criminals to establish subsequent accounts until this fraud is discovered. If your child's identity is stolen at an early age and not discovered until they become an adult, this excessive lapse in time makes it virtually impossible to determine where the initial identity theft fraud began.

Why Teens Fail...

Identity thieves rarely target a specific victim. If your child's identity is compromised, it will likely be the result of a randomly generated Social Security number that happens to match your child's ID.

What To Fix...

You can and should minimize risk by shredding personal records and taking other security steps, but you will need to get familiar with how to access information from the major credit reporting bureaus.

What Is Identity Theft?

Identity theft occurs when an individual pretends to be someone else by assuming another person's identity. Identity theft is typically committed in order to facilitate obtaining credit and benefits in another person's name. The identity theft victim can then suffer the consequences of being held accountable for the criminal's actions.

Identity theft is also a significant problem that affects us all economically. Annual losses associated with identity theft currently exceed $50 billion a year. All of that lost revenue by credit card companies and other financers is then passed along to you the consumer. This is reflected in higher prices, higher bank fees, and higher credit card finance charges to make up for this lost revenue.

While your personal information may mean the world to you, sadly, to the identity thief it means very little. The average stolen Social Security number sells for as little as one dollar. Obviously, this means identity thieves are stealing these numbers by the thousands in order to make it worth their while. Logically, stealing the Social Security number of a child as opposed to an adult will likely delay reporting and allow the thief to escape arrest and prosecution.

Although your identity may cost the illegal buyer little, it can be a very expensive proposition for you in more ways than just money. The average victim of identity theft will spend approximately 175 hours working to repair the damage done to their credit reports and their lives. Even after working hard to repair your damaged credit history, there is no guarantee the same troubles may not occur again. Once personal information has been compromised, it is exposed forever and available to other potential criminals for continual resale.

Why Teens Fail...

The average victim of identity theft will spend approximately 175 hours working to repair the damage that has been done to their credit reports. Teens are generally not equipped with the resources to handle this.

What To Fix...

Teach your teens about identity security and how to get a free credit report. Remember, an ounce of prevention is worth a pound of repair.

How Your Child's Identity Is Stolen

Long gone are the days when identity thieves have to go dumpster diving or steal mail out of your mailbox in order to obtain your personal information. With the advent of the Internet, now identity thieves can steal all of your personal information from the convenience of their own homes.

All of us have key pieces of information that can be found on the Internet, oftentimes available to anyone, free of charge. Online information records are available that cover birth, education, work, death, etc. A simple search of the various directories found on the Internet can reveal a treasure trove of information. Take a look at just a few of the following sites and see how much information is out there online in your own name:

Google.com
Brbpub.com
Zabasearch.com
Peoplefinders.com
Zoominfo.com
Archive.com
Birthdatabase.com
Thepaperboy.com
Searchsystems.net
Intelius.com
Melissadata.com
Publicrecordsonlinerecords.com
Myfamily.com
Ancestry.com

Even if you take advantage of some of these websites' offering an "opt out" (i.e., having your information removed from public view), it is important to remember that it is still nearly impossible to completely disappear from the Internet. It is important to remember that security through obscurity is no security at all.

Additionally, depending upon the age of your child, they are probably engaged in social networking, using various sites such as Facebook, Twitter, and Formspring. With the advances in technology, kids also do not have to wait until they are at home on their computers. Whether it is on their laptop, iPad, or smartphone, kids are posting information in a variety of places, rarely under the watchful eyes of parents. Often kids will post all sorts of information on their social networking pages, such as their age, date of birth, and home address, thereby giving would-be thieves an unprecedented advantage to steal your child's persona.

How to Detect If Your Child's Identity Has Been Stolen

How do you know if your child's identity has been stolen? First, it is a good idea to check with the Social

Security Administration once a year to make sure no one is using your child's Social Security number. A simple call can determine if your child's Social Security number has ever been used in the past, such as by someone using it to obtain employment.

Next, check your child's credit report, which can be done by calling each of the three major credit reporting agencies.

Equifax: 800-525-6285
Experian: 888-397-3742
TransUnion: 800-680-7289

Why Teens Fail...

Some would argue that it is already too easy for teens to get credit and ruin their own credit score. Now you have to worry about someone else ruining their credit!

When calling to check, if you discover some irregularity you can take this opportunity to report the potential fraud. By law, you are entitled to obtain a free credit report from each of the three reporting agencies once a year. It is recommended that you call only one of the agencies every four months, rotating each of them throughout the year. This way, you will be able to check on your child's credit report, as well as your own, three times a year rather than just one time.

Should your child start receiving pre-approved credit card offers or suspicious financial opportunities in the mail that otherwise would normally only be sent to adults, this is a clue that someone has been using their Social Security number.

What To Fix...

Rotate through the three credit bureaus every four months and request a free credit report. Also, call the Social Security Administration once a year and check your SSNs.

Furthermore, should you be contacted by a collection agency regarding an account in your child's name, it is a certainty that your child has been a victim of identity theft.

WTF

Protecting Your Child from Identity Theft

Armed with your child's personal information, such as a Social Security number, the identity thief then has enough information to apply for and obtain birth certificates, which is one of the most valuable of all of the identity documents.

A birth certificate is generally accepted by nearly all government agencies as definitive proof of identification. Birth certificates can easily be obtained both online and through the mail. There is no conformity with birth certificates, making it difficult to refute the authenticity. In the United States alone, there are currently more than eight thousand state and local government offices that are issuing more than ten thousand variations of the birth certificate.

Birth certificate documents can also be easily altered to reflect a different year of birth, making it easier to obtain through fraudulent means other real documents, such as a driver's license, passport, and other important documents that can impact your child's future. Imagine the potential damage that might occur should someone using your child's personal identifiers establish a criminal record in their name. Not only would it make it difficult for your child to obtain employment in the future, but he or she might also one day be mistakenly arrested by law enforcement based upon the criminal history committed the identity thief.

So what can be done to prevent your children from becoming victims of identity theft?

Once you have been issued your child's Social Security card, be sure to store it in a safe place, such as a safety deposit box. Also, only give out your child's SSN when it's absolutely necessary to do so. If you can provide an alternate form of identification, do so whenever possible.

Parents need to be equally careful when disposing of any personal information, including that of their children. Your trash could be a treasure trove of information for an identity thief. Before you dispose of information on paper or online, make sure no one else can obtain it for their own use.

Only dispose of your personal information in a safe and secure manner. Shred all letters, forms, and other paperwork that include your child's personal information before you throw these items away. To avoid the inadvertent online compromise of personal information, delete electronic computer files that you no longer need, and empty your online trash and recycle bin.

Likewise, learn how to remove personal or financial information that is stored on your computer, cell

Why Teens Fail...

Thieves will likely use your child's SSN to obtain a copy of the birth certificate. This will in turn be used to create a false driver's license or some form of state identification.

What To Fix...

Keep your family's documents in a safe place such as a fireproof safe or a safety deposit box at a remote location such as your bank of choice.

phone, or other electronic device before you dispose of it. Failing to do so leaves you vulnerable to others who might retrieve the information.

For years we have taught our children never to talk to strangers, but do they understand that everyone they meet on the Internet, no matter how friendly they may seem, is a stranger? As soon as they are old enough to understand, teach your child to never reveal personal information to anyone on the Internet, no matter how trustworthy that person may seem. This is especially important because the primary mode of communication amongst children has changed from talking on the telephone to communicating via the Internet. Once personal information is given out it has been compromised forever, and the Internet makes it easier and faster to share with more people than ever before. Kids need to know not to share personal information when asked, nor should they post personal information unnecessarily on their social networking sites.

Sadly, it is also important to remember that identity theft is frequently committed by persons other than just strangers. Many times these crimes are also perpetrated by persons who may be close to the family, or even may be related. Again, kids need to know to safeguard their personal data from everyone at all times, and this message is best taught by you the parent.

One added serious concern is that the theft of your child's personal information also has the potential to impact his or her physical safety. If your child is posting vacation pictures on their social networks while the family is traveling, this communicates to the general public that no one is home, or worse, where your child can be found. The same rules apply with your kids who are Tweeting from parties and posting simultaneously to their Facebook pages, letting their followers know where they are currently located.

> **Why Teens Fail...**
>
> *What did you do with your last old computer? Did you throw it away or donate it to charity? Either way, did you effectively delete all of your personal information from the hard drive?*

> **What To Fix...**
>
> *There are free utilities such as CCleaner that you can use to permanently remove deleted files from your computer hard drive. Download this or another reputable utility from a safe location and use it periodically.*

Even uploading photos from cell phones to social networking sites carries inherent dangers. Today's technology allows photos to record the physical address of where the picture was taken. If your child is uploading photos taken moments before at a friend's house, a potential predator can then find the exact address of where your child is by geo-locating them through this imbedded information.

Some Identity Theft Solutions

Consider the option of signing up your family members, to include all children, for a credit monitoring and identity protection solution. There are a number of reputable companies, such as Merchants Information Solutions, Inc. (800-966-0576, www.merchantsinfo.com), that will not only keep an eye on your credit report activity, but will also help you repair any damage that might occur. Lock down your child's credit report. You can contact each of the credit reporting agencies and request that their credit reports be locked; i.e., that no credit card, loan, etc., can be issued using their Social Security number. Locking down a credit report is free of charge, and there is only a nominal fee to unlock the credit report once again, which can be done when the child is own enough to begin building and establishing his or her own credit rating. If a criminal cannot use your child's SSN to gain approval for credit through the credit reporting agencies, your child's credit history cannot be compromised.

Children need to learn to use common sense when using the Internet, and that is more than not just talking to strangers. If a stranger approached your child and offered them a free game or video, they probably would not accept it. They must employ that same common sense when on the Internet. Teach your children not to accept unsolicited offers via the Internet and explain that this is one of the ways criminals are trying to steal their information.

Identity theft can occur online in the form of spyware, a type of computer program secretly installed on your computer that can read everything on your hard drive. To avoid having your computer infected by spyware, neither you nor your child should ever open an email attachment, regardless of who sent it, unless it is first scanned for viruses. Use a good software protection program and keep it regularly updated to ensure it is capable of defending against the most recent virus creations.

Just as important, your child must be careful to not visit unfamiliar websites that can be hostile. A hostile website is one that looks inviting, perhaps offering the opportunity to download a new game or look at cool pictures. However, the site has been set up to attract your child for the express purpose of secretly downloading hostile elements to your computer that can cause damage while extracting any private information held within.

Children also must learn to never share their passwords, enabling others to access their computers, email accounts, or social networking sites. Also, your child should have a strong password, making it difficult for someone to hack into the computer system. Do not use the names of pets or sibling for passwords, as these are the first things computer hackers will try when attempting to break into your system. Furthermore, most password hacking is not even done by an individual, but rather is performed electronically by sophisticated computer programs that are designed to try thousands of combinations per minute.

In creating a strong password that would be difficult to break, it is recommended that your child's password be a minimum of twelve characters. How is your child going to remember twelve characters? Easy.
A simple formula for creating a password that is virtually impossible to decode is by using a mathematical equation.

For example: 1999PLUS2001=4000

This simple password uses numbers, symbols, and both upper- and lowercase letters. You can use numbers that would be easy for your child to remember, such as the year of their birth along with their house number, to create a password equation such as above.

It is also important not to use the same password for every application. This way, if one password is by chance compromised, the identity thief will not have access to all of your other sites that might contain personal data. Again, there is no need to create unwieldy and complicated passwords. Rather, just slightly alter your password equation:

Why Teens Fail...

Posting too much information via social networking can give thieves just what they need to rob you blind. Your kids' phones can upload pictures from wherever they are, often including GPS information about their location.

What To Fix...

Don't inadvertently tell thieves where you are by posting your location when you are away from home. Turn off the GPS option on your cell phone to prevent posting locations with photographs.

1999PLUS2001=4000Facebook
1999PLUS2001=4000Gmail
1999PLUS2001=4000Yahoo

By simply adding the name of the program your child wishes to access to the end of their password equation, you have created a particularly unique password for every different computer function he or she needs to protect. All of these passwords are generally too complicated for either the individual trying to guess, or the complex computer program designed to hack.

A Word about Your Child's School

The FTC Consumer Alert advises that there are laws to help safeguard your child's and your family's personal information. For example, the federal Family Educational Rights Privacy Act, enforced by the US Department of Education, protects the privacy of student records. It also gives parents of school-age kids the right to opt out of sharing contact information with third parties, including other families.

If you're a parent with a child who's enrolled in school, the FTC suggests that you find out who within the school has been granted access to your child's personal information. Also, take steps to verify that your child's information is kept in a safe and secure location.

Pay close attention to any materials your child brings home from school, or are sent to you via mail or email, that request your child's personal information. You will want to find out how the school plans to use this information and if it is even necessary to provide. Opt out if you have the right to do so.

Schools are required to distribute and make available information that explains your rights under the federal Family Educational Rights Privacy Act. This act is designed to protect the privacy of your child's educational records. Furthermore, it grants you the right to inspect and review your child's education records, consent to the disclosure of information in the records, and correct errors that might be in the records. Take advantage of your rights under this act to ensure your child's personal information is both accurate and protected.

Inquire as to the directory information and distribution policy for your child's school. Generally, student directory information includes your child's name, address, date of birth, telephone number, email address, and even a school photo. All of this information makes potential identity theft relatively easy. Under the Family Educational Rights Privacy Act, schools must inform parents about the school's directory policy, and afford the parent the right to opt out if they wish to do so. As with most things, submitting your request to the school in writing will help you formally document your wishes to ensure the school complies with your request. Alternatively, if you do not choose to opt out, directory information may be available not only to the people associated with your child's school, but also to the general public—i.e., potential identity thieves.

Request to see the school's policy on surveys. The Protection of Pupil Rights Amendment gives you the right to see surveys and instructional materials before they are distributed to students. Again, this is a step to ensure your child is not unnecessarily providing personal information to others when there is no real need to do so.

Are there programs that occur on school grounds that are not affiliated with the school? Activities such as sports, music, and Scouting frequently make use of the school's facilities, yet have no official affiliation with the school district. These programs and activities may also have websites on which your child's name and picture can be displayed. Know the privacy policies of these organizations, and make sure you understand how your child's information will be used and shared with others.

If you school is the victim of a computer intrusion or some other data breach, be sure to take action. If the possibility exists that your child's personal information may have been compromised in some way, contact the school and ask to be fully informed of the breach and what actions they are taking in order to correct it. Talk with

Why Teens Fail...

Teens use weak passwords or no passwords at all. They often share passwords with friends. No. No. No.

What To Fix...

Create a password scheme that is not predicable or easily breakable by software algorithms. See suggestions on this page.

those associated with the school who are familiar with the incident and ask what they are doing to minimize or negate the damage. If you do not believe the necessary action is being taken, you can contact the Family Policy Compliance Office, US Department of Education, 400 Maryland Ave SW, Washington, DC 20202-5920.

What to Do If Your Child Becomes a Victim of Identity Theft

Unfortunately, despite everything you have just read, as the world continues to change and all of our personal data migrates to electronic form, the probability strongly exists that one day you or a member of your family may become a victim of identity theft. Nevertheless, there is a big difference in becoming a victim and allowing yourself to continue to be a victim. The following steps outline what to do should a member of your family become a victim of identity theft.

Immediately contact the Social Security Administration Fraud Hotline at 800-269-0271 to report that your child's Social Security number has been compromised. The Social Security Administration can take action to flag your child's SSN in the event that someone tries to get a new card issued for them. Not only will the criminal be prevented from receiving a Social Security card, the criminal's request might just provide enough information regarding their location to lead to an arrest.

After reporting the compromise to the Social Security Administration, contact the Federal Trade Commission at 877-FTC-HELP or 877-ID-THEFT, or online at www.consumer.gov. The Federal Trade Commission is the lead government agency in the collection of all information regarding the theft of personal information and often can assist other law enforcement agencies by providing additional information that might be helpful to their investigations.

If you determine that someone has fraudulently used your child's personal information to obtain a credit card, make a purchase, or obtain a loan, you need to contact all of the commercial account issuers in question. Call and ask for their fraud or security departments, or whoever handles fraudulent accounts. In today's day and age, every bank and business is familiar with identity theft and has established a department for these very instances. Make sure you inform them both by phone and in writing to ensure you have documentation of having reported the compromise. Likewise, make sure you specify that all such open accounts are fraudulent and should be closed immediately.

Next, contact your local police and insist that they take a report. Often, the police will advise that the FBI or some other agency investigates identity theft and that you should call them. Wrong! While there may not yet be enough evidence to open an ID theft investigation, your stolen identity was probably used to commit another more obvious crime. For example, the person who steals your child's identity and then fraudulently obtains a million-dollar loan might not be investigated for the identity theft, but rather for the bank fraud.

WTF

Needless to say, with the thousands of persons becoming victims of identity theft each month, law enforcement will investigate few cases, and even then only if the losses are generally in the millions of dollars. Nevertheless, you will want to make a police report to have proof that your child has been a victim as you work to repair their credit history. Notify the police in both the community in which you live and also in the community where the identity theft occurred. If you live in Arizona but learn your child's identity was stolen or is being used in California, notify the authorities in both locations. Get the police report number and later obtain copies of all of these police reports, which you will most likely need as you work with the credit reporting agencies in order to restore your child's credit report and future good credit.

Finally, keep a detailed log of all of your contacts and efforts pertaining to your efforts subsequent to discovering the identity theft. Note the locations called, the names and titles of the people you spoke with, and the date and time of the conversation. When calling, be sure to

Why Teens Fail...

You can take many steps to avoid having your identity stolen, but unfortunately, nothing is 100 percent foolproof. After all that you do, you or your child may still become the victim of ID theft.

What To Fix...

Call Social Security Administration Hotline: 800-269-0271.

Contact the FTC: 877-FTC-HELP

Contact the compromised account issuer and then file a police report.

ask what the procedures the company has in place to correct the situation and what is required of you to help them facilitate this. Document everything in writing and confirm in a letter to the companies that you had previously advised them of the identity theft. This way you will have proof of your efforts and put the company on notice that you have lived up to your legal responsibilities.

Learning More about Preventing Identity Theft

There are many websites that offer good information on preventing you and child from becoming victims of identity theft. Some of these sites are:

www.safeteens.com: information on keeping your teens safe

www.netfamilynews.com: free newsletter on the cyber issues affecting your family

www.safekids.com: information on keeping your kids safe

www.technorati.com: search engines to locate blogs that your child may be visiting

Finally, the following online website developed by Carnegie Mellon University offers a fun and interactive game that kids can play to teach them how identity thieves use the Internet to try and steal their personal information, and what your child can do to prevent it from happening:

cups.cs.cmu.edu/antiphishing_phil/quiz/index.html

What to Remember

Anyone can become a victim of identity theft, and because of their age, children may be the more desirable target.

Teach your children never to share their personal information with anyone unless they have your permission to do so.

Teach your children to be safe online and to recognize that the person they are communicating with may not be whom they claim to be.

Make sure your children understand that once they post their personal information online, it will be on the Internet forever.

Check your children's credit report regularly to determine if they have been a victim of identity theft.

If your child has been an identity theft victim, take the necessary steps to report to law enforcement and notify the appropriate agencies.

Armed with this information, you are now better prepared to try and prevent your family from becoming victims of identity theft. And should an identity theft occur, you now have the necessary tools to take positive action.

Why Teens Fail...

Repairing your identity and your financial reputation is a tedious and cumbersome project that takes patience and endurance. Some victims are tempted to just give up.

What To Fix...

Keep a file folder with detailed logs of every call you make and every person you talk to. Document your contact in writing to companies and investigative agencies. Remember there is a light at the end of the tunnel!

CHAPTER 5
MORE NIGHTMARES FROM THE NET
BY TANYA CORDER, POLICE DETECTIVE

I work in the sex crimes unit for my police department as a detective in the Internet Crimes Against Children (ICAC) task force. I have been arresting predators in this capacity since 2006. While there have always been bad people who want to hurt children and there seem to be more and more every year, I'm here to tell you that many of the child victims I come across could have avoided their ordeals by following a few simple tips. Allow me to share a few stories with you to underscore these suggestions for your family's safety.

> ### Why Teens Fail...
> *Sites like "Jailbaitgallery.com," while morally reprehensible to most parents, generally skirt the legal issue of child pornography by showing clothed images of minors with lewd discussions about them.*

My Ten-Year-Old, the Porn Star?

I was sitting at my desk one morning when I received a phone call. Sally (not her real name) was hysterical, and rightfully so. A family friend had called her with some pretty scary news: Sally's daughter's pictures were posted on a website called "Jailbaitgallery.com."

WTF

> ### What To Fix...
> *Understand that laws vary from state to state in defining exactly what constitutes child pornography (more appropriately referred to as images of minors depicted in sexually exploitative acts).*

Now why Sally's girlfriend was on this site...let's just say I decided not to ask. As I was talking to Sally, I went onto Jailbaitgallery.com to have a look for myself. My stomach churned. The site had hundreds of teen pictures that were uploaded by disturbed individuals, along with sick comments about these young girls and their body parts. I too am a mother, and the thought of my child's photo appearing on this site along with adults making sexual innuendos about her made me extremely angry. Jailbaitgallery.com is a place where anybody can upload a picture of a child and then multiple people can post their thoughts. Alongside the images of these children are adult pornography advertisements.

Many of you are asking yourselves, how did somebody get these children's pictures to upload onto a site such as this? I can tell you exactly how this type of thing happens. Using Facebook, Instagram, or another social network site of choice, one of the girls "friended" somebody they did not know. This unknown adult male then saved these girls' pictures onto his personal computer and uploaded them onto this site. Right-click on the image, copy, and save it. Once this has happened, the ten-year-old child has just lost control of his/her pictures. Harmless, right? That's not how these parents feel.

Just a Boy Trapped in a Man's Body

A mother called me to report that her thirteen-year-old daughter was talking to a "boy" in Utah. The teenager claimed that she and this boy were boyfriend and girlfriend. The mother believed this was harmless, being that the boy lived in Utah, and surely he wasn't going to come and visit her minor daughter, right? What thirteen-year-old boy drives or flies to Arizona to see a thirteen-year-old girl? This girl talked to this "boy" for several months. The mother became curious about her daughter's "boyfriend" when her daughter left her computer logged onto Facebook, and Mom saw the messages going back and forth. In reading the conversations she became very alarmed, as the conversations were very sexual in nature. Only then did the mother take this relationship seriously. She took it much more seriously after I told her that the boy was really a twenty-four-year-old man who was also a registered sex offender. Having an Internet boyfriend now seemed like a very bad idea.

Not the Daycare Shuttle

Imagine this scenario: A fourteen-year-old girl meets a boy on MySpace. This boy tells her how pretty and "hot" she is. The young girl is flattered, as she does not hear much positive reinforcement inside her home or elsewhere. This girl, who has very low self-esteem, is now told by a "boy" that she is pretty, hot, and sexy. She agrees to meet him in the parking lot after school so they can go somewhere to have sex. Fortunately, she also confides the plans to her best friend. The friend tells a school resource officer, who in turns watches the parking lot for a male with the description provided by the friend. The investigation reveals that the teenage girl met the man on MySpace. The man has been talking to the girl for several weeks about having sex with her and has sent her images of his penis. He is twenty-five years old and has a wife and newborn baby at home. Is this the type of encounter you would want your fourteen-year-old daughter to have?

> **Why Teens Fail...**
>
> *The Internet is the best playground in the world for predators to seek out children and teens with low self-esteem.*

WTF

Who's Your Sugar Daddy?

> **What To Fix...**
>
> *Spend lots of time building up your son's and daughter's self-esteem in order to minimize their need and desire to seek that social gratification from strangers.*

A fifteen-year-old teen confided to an adult friend that an adult friend he met on Facebook sexually victimized him. The adult "friend" was forty-seven years old. He had purchased this boy multiple expensive items but made it clear that nothing is for free. The adult male requested sexual favors for these items. The teenage boy, coming from a low-income family, did sexual acts on this man. I learned that this man had thirteen other victims, all from similar backgrounds. When the teenage boy wanted this to stop, the adult male threatened to tell the boy's parents. The child was terrified, as he was not gay and didn't want his father to hate him. He was brave enough to tell me his story, and a child predator is now in prison. The twelve other boys who were victimized by this man would not talk to me, and to this day, I still don't know who they are.

Eight Seconds of Fame

An anonymous report came in through the National Center of Missing and Exploited Children. The person reported that there was a girl at his high school who had made a nude sexual video of herself. I viewed the video, and if this had been my little girl, I would have been devastated. This video was about thirty seconds long. The girl was nude and masturbating herself. I found out who she was and asked why she would make such a video of herself. The girl said she'd met a man on Facebook and he had asked her to make the video. He'd said he would be the only one to watch it. The teen had no idea that he'd recorded the video. The video was now all over the Internet. This young lady was an honor student, had excellent grades, and wanted to be a teacher someday. I have since asked numerous principals if this young lady would have a hard time finding a job as a teacher someday. The answer from every one of them was yes. This eight-second mistake changed this teenager's future.

I could list case after case. Many of you reading this would say that this would never happen to your child. What we need to understand is that times have changed and we as parents have some catching up to do. In addition to the changes in technology, let's take a look at our economy. Many children no longer have a parent at home when they get home from school. Some families are struggling financially. Most two-parent households have both parents working. If you're a single mother or father, then you too are working. Being a parent becomes much harder. We get home from work and the last thing we think about is checking up on our children. As a single parent, I would come home from work and the very last thing I wanted to do after working ten stressful hours was to sit on a computer checking up on my teenager. But I am here to tell you that times have changed and we as parents need to change with the times.

I am the first person to say I love technology. But I have also learned through these criminal cases that technology carries with it a huge responsibility. In reading the cases above, many parents have a knee-jerk reaction. We want to protect our children, and the first thing that comes to mind is taking away the things that can possibly hurt our children. With technology, that's not really a realistic answer, as it is here to stay. My goal is to help you teach your children twenty-first-century responsibility to better ensure their safety and emotional well-being.

Social Networking and Privacy Settings

Let's start by discussing what you can do to better ensure your teen's safety online. We will begin by discussing social networking.

Facebook is one of the most popular social networking sites online today, though please understand that there are thousands of other social networking sites out there. We will discuss Facebook in this chapter, but the suggestions I make apply to other social networking sites as well. I will provide you with my suggestions and explain why I think they are helpful.

1. Know the rules of the social networking site. Facebook requires that you be at least thirteen years old to have an account with them.
2. Do not let your teenager post their picture on their profile.
3. Set up the privacy settings to ensure that your teenager is only communicating with people they know.
4. Talk to your children about being friends with people they know and have physically met in person.
5. Tell your children not to post pictures on Facebook that they wouldn't want their mother, father, coach, teacher, or neighbor to see.
6. Warn kids not to write anything on Facebook that they might later regret.
7. Develop a contract with your teenager on what they can and can't do on social networking sites.
8. Require your children to share their password with you—and only you.
9. Monitor your teenager's Facebook account.
10. If your teen has a Facebook account and you don't, learn how to use it.

Why Teens Fail...

An unprotected Facebook page to a sexual predator is like an unmanned candy store to a three-year-old.

What To Fix...

Use the privacy settings in Facebook to your full advantage. Don't accept friend requests from strangers, even if they appear like harmless kids on their profiles...

I have worked many cases where a child is ten or eleven and they have been victimized. I come to find out that the child had a Facebook account either that the parent didn't know about or that the parent actually helped the child set up. I understand that we want our children to have what other children have, but Facebook and other social networking sites have rules. Please read the rules and follow them. These are rules are implemented to protect your children.

I suggest that parents don't allow their children to post their actual photo as their profile picture. I personally don't feel that our teenage children need to have their picture out there with their name alongside of it for the

Not that long ago law enforcement would get called when a suspicious person was hanging out at the school looking at children, or they would get reports that a creepy man was checking out children at the playground. Law enforcement would respond to these calls and were able to identify who that person was and the reason they were at that particular location. With modern technology, we don't get as many of those calls. Why, you ask? Because our children are posting their pictures on social networking sites and providing predators with everything they need to know about them. They provide a picture, a name, what school they go to, what their interests are, who their friends are, and so on. Predators can simply "shop" for a child from their computer. They no longer need to look suspicious hanging out at schools, parks, libraries, or the mall. They can simply pick their child from the comfort of their home. Don't let someone shop for your child.

WTF

Privacy settings are put on many of these social networks to protect your children. Use them, but please don't think that just because your teenager has the privacy settings on that everything is safe. A stranger can still email your child requesting to be their friend. I will say this many times throughout this chapter: most of my cases come from a child friending someone they didn't know. It is not acceptable to add a friend because another teen says that they know this person and he or she is okay. Express to your teenager that they need to physically know the person they are talking to. Sit down with your teen periodically

Why Teens Fail...

Some parents are inclined to remove all access to the Internet from their teens. Knee-jerk reactions seldom solve long-term problems.

What To Fix...

Start by allowing limited access to the Internet under parental supervision. As teens demonstrate responsibility, try adding only a few privileges at a time until they again demonstrate responsibility.

and go through their "friends." Ask questions; find out whom your teenagers are talking to. If you check your teenager's friend list on Facebook and he or she has two thousand friends…that's a problem, right?

Do not post anything that you wouldn't want the world to see. That doesn't just apply to social networking, that's for the Internet in general. An eight-second video changed one girl's future. What we need to explain to our children is an inappropriate image could have not just legal consequences but also emotional consequences. Once an image is in cyberspace, you can't get it back. Talk to your teens about the legal and emotional ramifications of posting an inappropriate image. I do hundreds of presentations to teenagers. Your child either knows what sexting is, or she is about to find out from her peers. Sexting, in simplistic terms, is sending nude or seminude pictures via a cell phone or on the computer. We will talk more about sexting shortly.

> **Why Teens Fail…**
>
> *Sexting is the practice of sending nude images or videos via cell phone or webcam. Once an image is sent, it cannot be "unsent."*

I have heard countless stories about teenagers trying to obtain their first jobs, only to find out someone won't hire them because the perspective employer researched the teen online and found things that made them not want to hire the child. Your teen needs to know—I will say it again—is that once an image or video is out there, you can't get it back. Everything he does today via social networking could possibly be with him for the rest of his life. Encourage kids to use the Internet wisely so future doors don't shut on them.

> **What To Fix…**
>
> *Teach your teen to protect her digital reputation. Many a girl has been recorded, and files with compromising images or video can be easily uploaded to pornographic websites without her knowledge.*

Don't write anything on social networking that you could possibly regret. This goes hand-in-hand with the paragraph above. If your child has an issue with somebody or something, please tell them to discuss it appropriately, in person, or go to a trusted adult. You can't get the words back once they're posted online.

A Word about Contracts

Develop a contract with your child describing how they can use social networking and the Internet. Establish the rules so you both have a clear understanding of what the teen can and can't do. If the contract is broken, the teen has a clear understanding of why his or her privileges are being revoked. Many teens have already been exposed to an incident where somebody has made them feel uncomfortable online. I've asked hundreds of teenagers why they didn't report that incident to a parent or a trusted adult. The answer? "My parents would take away my cell phone or computer." Look around. The cell phone and computer are *huge* parts of our children's lives. Losing cell phone or computer privileges is a big deal to a teenager. I believe a contract creates a safe environment for children because they can come to you if something makes them uncomfortable and have less fear that you're going to take their computer or cell phone away.

Your teenagers are not calling the police when something makes them uncomfortable online. I have yet to receive a telephone call from a teenager. It is you the parent who make that call. I know it's scary when your child tells you something happened online and their safety could be at risk. Our knee-jerk reaction as a parent is to take the items away that could put our child in danger. It's a fine line as to how you respond to an issue such as this if it arises in your household. I stated in the beginning that you know your child better than anyone, and only you can make that decision if such a thing happens in your home. But have a plan as to how you are going to respond if something like that should ever happen. Make a plan that works for you to allow your child to feel safe enough to come to you if something makes them uncomfortable. If you're worried that you might lose your cool, tell your child to report it to their uncle, aunt, neighbor, or your best friend. However your child reported it shouldn't matter—at least they told somebody.

Why Teens Fail...

Teens often fail to report a risky encounter on the Internet for fear that their parents will revoke all Internet and cell phone privileges.

What To Fix...

Parents and teens should consider using an online behavior contract that outlines expectations for both parties. Also, parents should make it a point not to overreact when their kids report risky behavior.

A Word about Passwords and Privacy

Passwords are there for a reason. They allow only the account holder to log into their account and nobody else. If your teen has an account online, it is my belief that you as the parent should have the password. I have had the occasional parent say they feel their child should have some privacy. I do believe people need privacy, and when kids becomes adults, they can have all the privacy they desire. However, as a mother I believe my job is to protect my children and give them the tools they need to be successful adults. I grew up with a very nosy mother. She read my notes and would occasionally go through my bedroom, and as a teenager I resented that. But today I am grateful my mother did those things. I believe I avoided a lot of poor choices because I knew not much got past my mother. She was not my best friend. Her belief as a mother was to shape and mold me to make good choices. I didn't understand that then, but I do now. Our children have plenty of best friends at school. Let's not be our children's best friends. Our teens need parents.

Tell your child not to share their passwords with their friends. Friendships with children come and go. One minute they are best friends with someone, the next week they no longer like that person. I've had cases where two teenagers get into an argument and one of the teens logs into the other teen's account and writes inappropriate things about other friends. Tell your kids this can be avoided by simply never giving your password to anyone, not even your best friend.

Additionally, if your child has a social networking account, review it on a daily basis. These sites are enjoyable for adults and teenagers but they come with a great amount of responsibility. Know who their friends are and make sure your child is staying within your computer contract. If you don't know how to use the program they are using, then it is my belief that you should either learn how to use it, or they shouldn't be on it. So many repercussions could happen if your teen misuses a site, including emotional and criminal consequences. My question is, why wouldn't parents want to keep track of their teen's social networking? If you are not very computer literate, ask a friend, find a class, or look for a book that will guide you through. An even better suggestion, ask you teenager to teach you! Many parents will tell me they just don't have the time to learn. I

Why Teens Fail...

Key loggers and other parental control software can be too intimidating for some parents, and many teens can circumvent these protections if the parents are not techno-savvy.

What To Fix...

If you implement a parental control suite, learn how to use it and don't rely exclusively on the parental controls for your teen's safety. Constant vigilance is still mandatory!

challenge you to make the time. It is in the best interest of your child's safety and well-being.

The last thing I want to discuss is a key logger. A key logger is a software program that you can install in your teenager's computer. This program records the real-time activity of a computer to include keystrokes, screen captures, instant messages, and websites visited, to name a few. There are many different key loggers out there. If your teen has an additional Facebook account, you will find out about it. If your child has additional email address, you will have the user name and password. This is an extremely helpful tool. My suggestion would be not to let the teenager know it's on the computer. I came to this conclusion after talking to multiple teens who have told me that their parent put one on their computer and now they don't use that computer when they are checking the accounts that their parents don't know about. Regardless of whether you tell your teen or not, please tell your husband, wife, boyfriend, or significant other if you have this program on the computer. This tool is meant for protecting your children, not to spy on your significant other!

A Little Bit More about Sexting

I have mentioned sexting in this chapter and it's certainly worth talking about, as I get reports on a daily basis. Sexting ("sex" plus "texting") is the act of sending sexually explicit message or photographs, primarily between cell phones. There are many issues that arise when a teenager is sexting another teenager. If a nude or seminude is transmitted by your teen, he/she has no longer has control of that image. Once that image is out, it can never be taken back. Criminal and emotional ramifications can come from that one image. Ask your teenager how they would feel if an entire high school had a nude or seminude image of them. As adults, if this happened to us, we would be devastated. Now imagine how a thirteen- or fourteen-year-old teenager would cope with it. Now let's take the emotional aspect out of it.

Teenagers need to know many states have laws that pertain to sexting. Your child needs to understand that if they participate in this type of behavior, there could be legal ramifications.

WTF

What To Fix...

Try a Google search of your state laws and sexting. For example, "Arizona" plus "state laws" plus "sexting." You might have to dig a little, but getting informed is the first step to protecting your kids.

I have asked hundreds of teenage girls and boys why they would send a nude or seminude image to somebody. The answer? Peer pressure. Please have an open line of communication with your children. Talk about sexting. Help them understand that one image could change the course of their life. Many teenagers have already made this bad decision and have suffered the consequences. We have read in the paper about children taking their own lives because they couldn't deal with the scorn and humiliation that occurred at school because their sexting image was going around the high school. Many of you are thinking, "Well, my child would never do that." The question I have then is why am I getting so many reports of it? Here are some suggestions to better ensure that this does not happen to your child.

Why Teens Fail...

Many parents and teens are not aware of the legal consequences of sexting behavior. It varies from state to state, with varying degrees of severity in regards to punishment.

1. Talk to your teenagers about sexting. Make sure they know of the personal and legal ramifications.
2. Explain to the teen that if they receive an image of sexting, they can do one of two things: they can delete the image or report it.
3. Contact your cell phone service providers. Request picture messaging be shut off.
4. Establish consequences.
5. Set up rules on texting.
6. Check their messages daily.
7. Talk about modesty.

We have already discussed communicating to your children about sexting. But what happens if your teenager receives an unsolicited sexting image? The teen has a couple of choices to avoid legal ramifications if they are caught with the image. They can delete the image or report it. Each state has different laws. I encourage you to find out what the law is in your state and make sure your child

Why Teens Fail...

Most sexting incidents happen late at night in the teen's bedroom.

What To Fix...

Enforce safety rules in your home such as no Internet in the bedroom, and all cell phones should be plugged in by 10 pm in the parent's room.

has a clear understanding of what to do if it happens to them.

Contact your telephone service provider. Most service providers can shut off picture messaging at your request. This will ensure your teen will not receive a sexting image on their cell phone, nor can they send one out. This seems to work really well, but please understand that sexting can also be done using a computer webcam or other photo upload software.

Have a cell phone contract with your teenager or include its use in the computer contract. Make sure they know what the rules are up front. If the contract is broken, the child will have a clear understanding of why their cell phone was taken away.

Set up rules for when your teenagers can text and when they can't. Check your phone bill to have a better understand how often your child is sending and receiving messages. In many households I have seen parents say no texting during dinner or when engaged in conversations with other family members. The best rule I have seen is that cell phones go into the parent's bedroom at night. Make your rules and stick with them.

Know how to use your child's cell phone. Check their messages and pictures and check them daily. Contact your service provider and find out if they provide a service where you can see the messages your children are sending and receiving.

Most important, talk to your children about modesty. Your teenager should think twice about taking his or her clothes off and standing nude in front of someone. A child's body is not something to exploit. Teach them to respect their bodies and their personal reputations. Many teenagers do things with their phones and their computers that they would never do in "real life." Encourage your child to spend less time texting and more time actually talking to their friends.

Concluding Thoughts of a Police Detective

Today's American teenagers are enveloped by technology. Many parents find themselves faced with difficult decisions when their child enters the teenage years. One of the biggest questions is how much technology does my child need, and at what age do I provide these tools?

During the last five years of investigating Internet crimes against children, two issues involving your children's safety come to my mind. You can save yourself a great deal of grief if you will just ask yourself these two questions: "Who are my children talking to on social networking sites?" and "What types of images are they receiving and sending on their cell phones?"

CHAPTER 6
DRUG USE: BEHAVIORS AND NORMS
BY STEPHANIE SIETE, DRUG EXPERT

As a drug expert in the field of prevention and education for over ten years, I have seen and heard plenty of stories about drug experimentation, addiction, and death. The stories have different outcomes, yet common denominators include early use, hurting loved ones, lying, stealing, inconsistent behavior, and acting in an out-of-control and disrespectful manner. Sadly, I have become desensitized to the horrible effects and endings. It is almost my norm, because it's what I have been exposed to regularly in the last decade.

I spend most of my days educating the community—parents, teachers, police, fire, probation officers, college students, healthcare workers, etc.—about the latest drug trends, how to recognize the signs of use, the behaviors associated with drugs, and what to do if you suspect use, and then sharing resources on how to prevent, intervene in, or treat the situation.

Parents and educators always want to pick my brain about what to do to get through to their kids. They all invite me to their schools and homes to talk to their teens. They can't imagine ever being as effective as I might be because of my "drug expert" title. I promise, just taking the time to learn a little more about the world of a teenager—what's normal to them, the drugs that are being sold in their high school and online, who their friends are and aren't, how they are feeling—and further asking questions and listening to them about their passions and hobbies will be more effective than I can ever be. The one thing a parent has with their kid that I don't have is time.

> **Why Teens Fail...**
>
> *Teens are exposed to "normalized" drug use behaviors on television shows and commercials, on the Internet, in music, and daily with teen friends.*

> **What To Fix...**
>
> *Be involved. Know what they are watching and who they spend time with. Talk about what the expectations and norms are in your home.*

WTF

People often think the topic of drugs is scary or not relevant to them. They might even think they know enough because of their drug experiences years ago, which I can guarantee are not the same as today. Many people still wear blinders and think the drug issue doesn't apply to them, so I spend a lot of my time getting them to buy into the fact that it is a community problem impacting all of us.

There are many drugs, illegal and legal, that one could use, so many it's nearly impossible to discuss or learn them all. They are ever-changing. Instead of learning each drug, learn the types of drugs, their health risks, and the signs/symptoms of use, and be able to explain in simple terms the truths about what they can do to a person's body, life, career, friends, and family. Being "real" about the impact of drug use and sharing real-life situations will keep a young person interested in what you are saying.

But don't do all the talking...LISTEN.

Let's examine some of the social barriers that allow our kids to become so knowledgeable about drugs and other risky behaviors. Identifying and understanding the problems, becoming an informed and involved parent, will better prepare you for some of the uncomfortable and necessary conversations that lie ahead with you and your teen.

Why Teens Fail...

Teens are young and impressionable. They are influenced by movies, celebrities, TV shows, Internet videos, peers, and family.

What To Fix...

Be the positive influence they need. Demonstrate healthy behaviors in eating, drinking, taking medication, etc. Teens watch and learn from what they see. Limit TV and Internet time. Fill their time with you.

Overexposure and the Normalization of Drugs

I do not believe all teens use drugs. However, I do believe they are all exposed to opportunities to learn what to use and how to use it. Social media websites like Facebook, video websites such as YouTube, the popularization of reality television, and risqué themes in current music have "normalized" a lot of substance abuse behaviors.

At the beginning of 2012, various sources estimated that there are over 800 million people with Facebook accounts. Many of these accounts belong to teenagers. People have the opportunity to befriend anyone from around the world, post personal pictures and videos, be tagged by others in pictures and videos, and say anything they want. Sound scary? Keep in mind that all of this material now belongs to Facebook, lives in Cyberland, and can be viewed forever. On top of that, parents have to deal with the teen brain, which is lacking development, life experience, and the ability to make good judgment calls (even when their brains are healthy and not chemically impaired).

Another source of media that is regularly used by people of all ages is the video site YouTube. It might be fun to watch music videos and catch up on television shows, but one can also view all the millions of personal videos posted daily by anybody with a camera. Take a minute to search any drug you have heard about and you will most likely find out how to use it and make it, what the drug looks like, and how the user behaves while under the influence.

Why Teens Fail...

Parents aren't educated on the truths and facts of drugs; therefore they can't/don't have necessary conversations with their teens.

Do you remember when you were able to watch TV as a family? There were quick thirty-minute shows focused on minor family issues that were appropriate for all of us to view together. Depending on when you grew up, you may have seen *The Brady Bunch, The Cosby Show, Full House, Family Ties, Growing Pains, Family Matters*…the list goes on and on. Fast-forward to today and we have TV shows glamorizing teen sex, sex with multiple partners, underage and excessive drinking, pill-popping, and foul language. The themes have changed and so have the titles: *Teen Mom, 16 and Pregnant, Jersey Shore, Gossip Girl, The Bachelorette, Battle of the Exes*, etc.

What To Fix...

Get educated. Read books, watch documentaries, go to trainings, and then use what you learn to ask open-ended questions to your teens.

Have I got you thinking about the many ways teens are easily exposed to dangerous drugs, behaviors, and trends? Again, I remind you that I do *not* think all kids do drugs, but there are definitely too many ways for them to see them, obtain them, and start using.

Drug Use in Your Home

You have heard it before: you don't need to know a drug dealer to get high. Some of the most dangerous drugs now come from our houses, yet another sign of how times have changed. If you think about it, we have always been aware of liquor cabinets and the ability to sneak some alcohol out of a bottle only to replace it with some water. However, that is not the only cabinet in the house a parent needs to monitor. Prescription medication is commonly abused, and the number one place to obtain it is from the medicine cabinet of a friend or family member. A lot of the missing medication goes undetected. I mean, who is going to notice if two or three pills are taken from a bottle of thirty? The majority of people don't take the time to count the exact number of pills in each container. Maybe we should.

Paints, glues, markers, Wite-Out, cleansers, aerosols, and gasoline are but a few of the household chemicals that may be found in a garage, kitchen, or office cabinet. These poisonous substances can be deadly with the first use. They smell different or strong and can produce lightheadedness, dizziness, and blurred vision. Worse, they can even stop the natural flow of oxygen from entering the brain, causing brain damage or death. Monitor these cabinets as well as those liquor and medicine cabinets.

We haven't even left our homes yet and already we are identifying numerous substances that can be abused, addictive, and deadly.

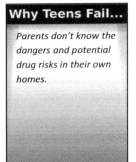

Why Teens Fail...

Parents don't know the dangers and potential drug risks in their own homes.

What To Fix...

Monitor the number of pills in containers. Lock up medications. Hide toxic chemicals and cleaners. Store alcohol out of everyday view.

Conversations from the Classroom

Speaking to students directly and honestly with a caring heart about the reality of drug use has produced many teachable moments, for me and the attendees.

I remember early in my career meeting a sixteen-year-old boy in a local high school who was not fond of my visiting his fifty-minute science class. He judged me when he saw the words "Drug Awareness and Education" projected on a screen. He rolled his eyes and mumbled something along the lines of "Why do we have to listen to this again?" I knew I had a challenge before me—and I loved it! I began my brief talk about the truths of what smoke does when you inhale it into your lungs on purpose. I explained it is a poison and too much of it over a period of time can cause death. He fake-coughed and said, "Bullshit." I didn't acknowledge him. I proceeded to talk about alcohol abuse and the toxicity of mixing other substances. I talked about our unique bodies and how they all respond differently, but in general you increase risks and damages to your health by using chemicals, especially at an early age when you are still developing. He blurted out, "Why do we have to listen to this crap?!" The teacher then stated, "Keep it up and you are out of here!" I looked at her and him and said, "Nope. He is fine." I thought to myself, he is not getting out of here this easy and whether he likes it or (clearly) doesn't, he is stuck with me.

> **Why Teens Fail...**
>
> *Parents talk, get angry and yell, and tell kids what they are doing wrong and how to do it right. In turn, kids start to tune them out.*

> **What To Fix...**
>
> *Listen to your teen without judgment. Ask questions, and don't give your opinion, yell, criticize or interrupt. Just LISTEN. Take note of feelings and reasons and try to understand and discuss calmly.*

I seemed to grab this kid's attention when I started talking about inhalants and products like nitrous oxide. I reported that inhaling poisons into your lungs on purpose is so dangerous that it can kill a first-time user because it blocks oxygen from entering the brain, causing lightheadedness, dizziness, blurred vision, and possibly even fainting. From this point forward, the student listened to the rest of my explanations. I remained factual and descriptive about how and why the body feels a certain way when a foreign substance enters it. I also shared lots of stories.

The bell rang. Most of the students bolted for the door. A few of them said thank you to me. This was when I noticed that the boy who had interrupted and challenged me in class was walking toward me. I admit I was a little nervous. My nervousness turned to surprise when he reached his hand out to shake mine. He said, "Thank you for coming to our class today. Are you serious about 'noz'?" I knew his slang term meant nitrous oxide and I responded with "Yeah. Why? Does it make your head hurt?" He nodded. "Yes, massive headaches." I explained that was because he was replacing his body's natural oxygen with poisonous nitrous oxide. It was killing brain cells, causing the headaches and blackouts. His body wasn't used to those chemicals and was reacting. He looked at the teacher and actually said, "You need to have her come back to our classes. Kids need to hear it the way she explained it. If I had known half of the shit she just said, I wouldn't have done half of it."

That was an eye-opening and memorable day for me. I will never forget the lessons learned for both of us. I will never know everything about drugs. You won't, either, but if you take the time to learn why drugs cause certain conditions and discuss it in a passionate and honest manner, you may be surprised at the outcome. I know I was.

Another incident in the classroom that comes to mind doesn't have to do with a particular drug; it's more about adults and the influence they have on young developing people.

I met and angered a middle school boy at an alternative school when talking about drug use and potential risks. I was stating the usual facts about harming your body and the impact abuse can have on loved ones when a boy screamed out at me, "What the hell are you supposed to do when you are eight years old and your uncle gives you a marijuana joint to smoke?!" At first I calmly replied, "It's unfortunate that you had that experience, that an important adult in your life misguided you so early."

WTF

The kid was clearly mad and further stated, "When everyone else in your family is doing it and you don't know any better, that's what you do!" He went on about how smoking pot wasn't a big deal. He did it with his uncle and brother and friends and they were fine. I told him he didn't have to follow what they did, or what anyone else did, for that matter. He yelled, "Are you telling me my family is wrong!?"

I probably didn't give the most soothing and professional response when I passionately snapped back, "There are other paths in life. There are other ways of seeing and doing things. I am sorry you haven't been exposed to them. That sucks for you. Maybe that is why

---

Why Teens Fail...

Teens don't have enough positive adult role models in their lives.

What To Fix...

It does take a village to raise a child. Kids need to hear messages over and over and from different sources. Have many adult role models in their lives: aunt, coach, neighbor, teacher, pastor, grandparent, counselor, school police officer, etc.

you met me today—maybe you need to see and hear from another adult role model who has a different view of drug use. You may be using drugs now, but no one says you have to continue to do so. You get to meet people like me who will challenge your thinking, get you to see different life paths. It's up to you which one you choose."

Though I was afraid of his response and shocked by mine, from that moment I had the class's attention and we had an amazing discussion about life and the importance of making good decisions regarding drugs and other subjects. Again, just listening, being honest and real, proved to leave an impression on both student and teacher.

The Rule of Five

Before we get into what some call the "gloom and doom" drug facts, let's think about some of the other ways we can have positive influences on our youth as adults.

Ask yourself: How old is my child? What do I want them to know five years from now? Should they know about sex? Suicide? Drugs? Cutting? Violence? *Start talking.*

Kids are more likely to listen to you and believe you in their pre-adolescent, formative years. You are their influence; what you do and say will be watched and listened to carefully. The next time you have a headache and are about to pop those pills into your mouth, consider going into the bathroom and engaging in that behavior behind closed doors where your child will not witness what you are doing. I promise you, if you swallow pills in front of them frequently and state you don't feel well or have a headache, they will start to mimic you. "Mommy, I don't feel good. Can I have a pill?" "Daddy takes a pill to help him sleep... can I have one?" "I have a headache...I need a pill." Plenty of parents have shared stories about three-year-olds asking these questions. I am a big fan of prevention, and displaying appropriate behavior and engaging in open communication is a great start.

Don't forget that by the time your child reaches middle school, they are going to be influenced by their new friends. The children are entering their teen years. Hormones are kicking in. They aren't seeing things as black and white or right and wrong. They are starting to see things as gray or as "maybe." Suddenly (and no offense), parents aren't as cool as they once were. All the more reason your early behaviors and conversations are so important.

Educators and field experts advise you to start talking to your child around the age of five about drugs. Yes, five. That may sound really early, but I am not suggesting you start off by asking a five-year-old about crystal methamphetamine. Instead you may have a conversation about taking pills. The talk may sound like, "Mommy/Daddy takes one of these pills when she/he feels really sick, but I would never take more than one pill because that is dangerous."

Doesn't this sound like an important and appropriate discussion for a parent and child? You will want to make sure these life-skill talks occur early and often. You can continue to build on the subject as your child ages and matures. That way, the drug talk never seems unusual if you have been doing it over the years. And even if it seems uncomfortable for you, I'll bet you'd rather the uncomfortable talks about drugs, sex, and suicide come from inside the home than outside it.

Adult Role Models

Notice I said "adults," not parents. As we have already heard, children are easily influenced by the adults around them. It is not just the parent that matters, but the neighbor, aunt, teacher, coach, pastor, employer, counselor, etc. who will also impact the youth. Keep positive role models around your kids. The more they hear healthy and wise messages from multiple sources, the bigger the influence. Teens will hear a lot of mixed messages from friends and probably be offered substances as well. If the teen has heard the consequences, the health risks, and the truth from Mom, Dad, teacher, neighbor, Uncle Jack, cool cousin Kelly, neighbor Jacki, the message may stick as it has been so repetitive.

Push Kids toward Their Passions

The number one reason teens are trying drugs today is because they are bored. They think there is nothing to do. How many times have you heard them say, "I'm bored." Don't worry, just be prepared.

By the time kids are in elementary school or middle school, I'll bet you've seen or know something they love to do. Do they like to sing? Dance? Write? Play with pets? Take pictures? Care for others? When you notice what they love or are passionate about, use it. Enroll them in that dance class. Sign them up for a photography class. Have them volunteer at an animal shelter or healthcare site. Keep them involved and driven by engaging them in their passions. It will steer them away from risky behaviors, and keep them busy and focused on their future. This alone may prevent them from engaging in drug use.

Why Teens Fail...

Kids are bored. According to Partnership for Drug Free America, the number one reason kids try drugs is boredom.

Heroin Is a High School Drug of Choice

Before sharing some stories and facts about heroin, I want you to understand 100 percent that prescription painkillers like Oxycontin are known as the legal form of heroin; they are interchangeable drugs. I know that over the years heroin has been considered a dangerous and deadly drug. It seemed to always have that negative stigma, but in recent years it has gained popularity and almost become "common sense" for an opiate addict to use. Let me explain…

What To Fix...

What is your kid passionate about? Do they love to sing? Dance? Take pictures? Care for animals? Use these passions to enroll them in classes or volunteer opportunities. It will fill their time and perhaps prevent chances to engage in risky behaviors.

Prescription Painkillers

We are an overprescribed society obsessed with managing our pain. If a kid has their wisdom teeth removed, they are offered everything from Vicodin to Oxycontin—no more ibuprofen and water, but some powerful painkillers. Doctors advise patients to use and finish the prescription in its entirety. This sets up a patient for dependency and addiction—either that or a sales opportunity, as one will quickly find out the high street value of these pills.

Prescription opiates (Vicodin, Percocet, Hydrocodone, and Oxycodone) will alleviate pain, but continual use can also build up a tolerance. For example, the two-pill dosage prescribed feels good, but the individual thinks three or five might feel better. Next thing you know they are using seven to ten pills a day and not even thinking about it. They will definitely notice if they try to stop using, though. The body would go through withdrawal and begin its own detox.

WTF

How do you feel right now? Are you feeling okay? Not sick? Are you able to go about your day? If so, you might be able to say you feel normal. But if you started altering your body's chemistry by taking daily painkillers, your body would adjust to a whole new level of normal. It would be used to or dependent on the medication it expects to feel okay. Let's say you want to stop using drugs, either because you can't afford them anymore or are forced to quit. Your body will react with physical changes such as sweating one minute and freezing the next, projectile vomiting, diarrhea, and muscle and bone pain. Sounds terrible, doesn't it? These are the symptoms of your body trying to change its "normal." Sadly, this detox or withdrawal will last for seven to ten days, and most people get even sicker a few days into it. This is how I usually explain to a teen why it is just best to never start, and then they won't have to go through this.

Using opiates and experiencing these symptoms is dangerous to the respiratory system. Most users will learn when they stop using the true meaning of "hell week" when they begin the withdrawal process. The problem is the user will feel so sick, many will desire the continued use of the drugs. If they do start up again, this is considered relapse and unfortunately is pretty common with physically addictive drugs.

The addict is desperate to keep using opiates and feel normal, but tends to learn it's hard to keep up with the addiction financially. On the street, an Oxy pill can run anywhere from twenty to eighty dollars a pill.

Why Teens Fail...

Prescription drugs are accessible and overprescribed. There is a theory they are safe because they come from a doctor. They are physically addictive and prevalent.

What To Fix...

Teens need to know the prescription painkillers are as addictive as heroin, and taking prescription pills early and often can start a physical addiction— a need to use daily—and lead to respiratory failure or early death. Pills should be used in moderation and only when necessary.

What's Next? Heroin.

This is where heroin use may come into play. Now that you understand how physically addictive other opiates like prescription painkillers are, you better understand the connection to heroin. The biggest draw to heroin is usually the affordability.

If a person is using ten-plus forty-milligram Oxy pills a day, this could be a $250–$400 a day habit. However, the amount of heroin needed to achieve the same effect will only run you about $40–$80 a day. Heroin is more potent than it's ever been, but it's also a very cheap drug to purchase.

Heroin used to be known as the dirty drug that people injected into their veins and which could cause infection. But in recent years, heroin has gone from 3–5 percent pure in the early 1980s to about 60–90 percent pure today. The high purity levels eliminate the need to inject the drug. You could smoke or snort it and still receive quite a euphoric high. Sadly, you also have a pretty good chance of killing yourself the first time you use it. That, or becoming an addict immediately.

> **Why Teens Fail...**
>
> *Drug addiction causes desperation and hurtful behavior.*

Energy Drinks Vs. Alcohol Energy Drinks

> **What To Fix...**
>
> *A drug addict is selfish because he only thinks about himself. He steals from loved ones, curses and screams at them, and engages in criminal activity to support his drug habit. Addicts' minds aren't clear and they engage in risky and selfish acts.*

In recent years the energy drink industry has spread like wildfire. Unlike cigarettes, alcohol, or even lottery tickets, you don't have to be of a certain age to buy them. Kids can't get their hands on them fast enough. Downing an energy drink can give kids an extra boost of energy to get through the school day, practice, or marathon Xbox sessions. These drinks allow kids to extend the night way past their regular bedtime.

Energy drinks contain high doses of caffeine, ginseng, guarana, taurine, and other stimulants. A 2011 report in the *Journal of Pediatrics* found that one energy drink is equivalent to four to five cans of soda. Effects of consumption can be increased heart palpations, seizures, strokes, and sudden death. When a young body and mind is developing, it is concerning to have all of these chemicals entering the system.

A recent US study of over four thousand students surveyed about their drinking habits found that those who drank energy drinks mixed with alcohol were more likely to suffer injuries, require medical help, or have sexual incidents relating to alcohol. The researchers concluded their findings were due to the fact that the energy drinks masked the feelings and obvious signs of drunkenness. Users can't tell if they're drunk, and they can't tell if someone else is drunk. Independently of this study, there was already concern and controversy in the United States regarding the packaging of alcohol energy drinks. Critics argued that not only were several health risks attached to them, but the appearance and packaging of the drinks also appealed to the underage drinker, and confused the consumer as to which drinks are alcohol and which are not.

Why Teens Fail...

Teens are consuming massive amounts of energy drinks, unaware of the ingredients in the products that can be harmful in large amounts.

Energy drinks typically have a nutritional or supplemental label listing their ingredients, calories, sugars, etc. Take note of that, as the alcohol energy drinks usually do *not* have this label. They just have their marketing decals on the can. This may help you better identify which cans contain alcohol and which ones do not.

What To Fix...

Teens' bodies and brains are developing. Know the ingredients—caffeine, ginseng, guarana, taurine, etc.—and the risks associated with them, like cardiac conditions, increased blood pressure, and seizures. Limit consumption.

Keep in mind that the average can of beer contains 4 percent alcohol and many of these alcohol energy drinks contain 7–12 percent. This is equivalent to a bottle of wine in some cases—a bottle of wine mixed with multiple sources of caffeine. That's a potentially risky and sickening combination.

What Are Synthetic Drugs?

Maybe you have heard the names Spice, K2, Bath Salts, Ivory Wave, or Jazz, to name a few. Chemically altered manmade substances, or synthetic drugs, are currently popular and, even worse, legal. They are derivatives of the illegal drugs (heroin, marijuana, cocaine, etc.), the only difference being a molecule or two in their chemical structure. These are designer drugs readily available to the public, with effects similar to those of dangerous substances, and the long-term effects are not yet known.

People are literally risking their lives when they try these synthetic substances. The drug Spice, sold as a potpourri or incense, can cause nausea, seizures, vomiting, and hallucinations. It is marketed as synthetic marijuana, yet the effects are much more severe. Bath Salts, which look like crystals, are commonly snorted like cocaine but contain the stimulants mephedrone, methylone, and/or methylenedioxypyrovalerone (MDPV). They can cause heightened temperatures and heart rates, leading to intense hallucinations and paranoia that can last for two to three days. According to many reports, the long-lasting paranoia produces suicidal tendencies and attempts. Keep in mind, these are just the symptoms that are visible to the eye. No one actually knows what is happening internally or what the long-term health effects are.

> **Why Teens Fail...**
>
> *Synthetic drugs are accessible and legally purchased online or in gas stations and head shops. Young people use them because they can obtain them legally.*

How Will I Know If Someone Is Using Synthetic Drugs?

> **What To Fix...**
>
> *Legal doesn't mean safe. Parents and teens need to know this and make decisions based on the unknown. It is unknown what the long-term effects of these drugs are. No one knows the exact effects or if damage is irreversible.*

The health hazards are horrible and would deter many, but customers are lured in by the sheer fact that these drugs are legal and accessible. Some of the chemicals used to produce Spice and Bath Salts have been banned federally or by individual states, but there are hundreds of chemicals one could use to duplicate the drug recipe. As a result, another major concern is the inability to detect these chemicals in a drug test. Sold on the Internet or in smoke shops, some of the products have labels on their packaging directing the buyer to purchase the product without the banned chemicals.

These obstacles—inaccurate drug testing, immediate health risks, accessibility, and unknown long-term effects—are ingredients for a scary or even deadly outcome. Keep in mind that just because the new drugs are legal, that does *not* mean they are safe. Synthetic drugs will continue to be produced and available, so it's important to stay knowledgeable and share what you know to inform others. Remind our youth that if they don't know what it is or what it will do, then it is best to avoid it. We have one life and many opportunities to make it a good one or a bad one. It all comes down to choices. Hopefully we make the best ones.

Drug Use Is Cyclical

Trying to decide what drugs to describe or inform parents about is a tough task. Drug use is constant. It has never just ended. The popular drugs change and usually resurface over time. I have chosen to highlight some of the current and prevalent drugs of concern going into 2013. I know this will change, and that's why I ask you to stay constantly informed and knowledgeable about trends, behaviors, and use.

Behaviors of Drug Use

There is no right or wrong way to do drugs. People eat them, snort them, drink them, smoke them, inject them, and, if you really want to be creative, you can insert them anally or vaginally. That said, go back to what I shared about being overexposed to information on the Internet. Not only does the Internet show you how to use, so do actual human examples, and television and movies obviously broadcast drug use too. If you have a child who snorts or smokes candies and food (it happens more than you think), I would suggest correcting them and talking to them about what is inappropriate versus what is appropriate. I have seen many addiction-type shows that have showed how to hide a foil-wrapped pill in your pocket, open that foil, and light the pill from below. Movies have shown how to take a beer bong made of funnel and tubing and how to stick it into your friend's butt and pour beer or other alcohol through it. You can even see how to light and smoke bongs on YouTube. Don't believe me? Check it out for yourself.

Resources, Tips, and Suggestions

I know this is a lot to digest and we still haven't even covered the details on stimulants, legal and illegal. There is much to be said about methamphetamine and cocaine as well as their legal counterparts, Adderall and Ritalin. Keep in mind, you can take what you know about prescription medications and energy drinks and apply it here. Don't overcomplicate it or stress about learning it all. Again, that isn't possible. What's important is that you know the risks and the trends. And the biggest factor is that you discuss it openly with your child.

Keep asking your teen questions. Use news stories and current events to start the conversation. Ask, "Have you ever heard of that at your school?" "What do you know about that?" Ask your kids to tell you what they know. Inquire about their friends. "Which friends are the biggest risk takers?" Know their best friends, not just neighborhood friends. There are plenty of websites that are helpful too. Three that I recommend are:

TimetoTalk.org
JustThinkTwice.com
TheAntidrug.com

Final Thoughts

Many people engage in risky behaviors because they don't feel loved or appreciated. *Build up the love and support for your teens.* Let them know they are loved by you and point out the other safe adult role models they can go to.

Remind teens that *drug abusers are selfish.* Drug users only think about themselves. They think about how they feel and want to feel. The steal and hurt others because their focus is drugs. Let kids know the impact is greater. Family and friends are hurt by drug use. Always work on getting teens to see the bigger picture and look long-term.

Legal doesn't mean safe. I can't say this enough. Remind kids of this. Let them know synthetic drugs are new to the scene and that research about the immediate

> **Why Teens Fail...**
>
> *Teens are always looking to fit in, be recognized, and feel good about themselves. Some of them change the way they feel by abusing drugs.*

> **What To Fix...**
>
> *Love them and make sure they know this. Don't just tell them, but show them. People who feel love and love their lives will reduce their risks and see more of a future life as opposed to living in the moment.*

and long-term effects is lacking. Remember that alcohol and prescription drugs are legal and some of the most deadly drugs out there.

Remember that life has no guarantees. *The decisions we make create our consequences.* Because life is unknown, we should focus on what we do know. Reduce our risks, make healthy decisions, and try to extend our opportunity to live.

A young, developing teen brain mixed with drugs is a chemistry experiment: you never know what you will get. It is a risk every time.

Prioritize this life. You only have one.

CHAPTER 7
DATE RAPE AND SEXUAL ASSAULT
BY BROOKE SCRITCHFIELD, SVU POLICE DETECTIVE

Merriam-Webster's American Dictionary defines date rape as "rape committed by the victim's date." Wikipedia defines it as "an assault or attempted assault usually committed by a new acquaintance involving sexual intercourse without consent." Both definitions make reference to this type of assault, also referred to as "acquaintance rape." Both of these definitions don't take into account other factors that are prevalent in reported cases of date or acquaintance rapes. The victim is not always on an actual traditional "date" with the perpetrator, the perpetrator is not always a "new acquaintance," and, contrary to popular belief, the victim is not always drugged. Since there are many forms of "sex," being a victim of date rape also does not mean there is always intercourse.

Like a lot of other sexually based crimes, date or acquaintance rape is often misunderstood, minimized, and frequently ignored. Over the past thirty-plus years, this type of assault has been gradually acknowledged as a tangible problem in society. Prior to this emergence of a new thought process, it was largely considered not to be rape if there were unwanted sexual advances or intercourse while on a date or with someone the victim knew. It is not always the stranger who is hiding in the bushes and waiting to attack you who rapes. In the majority of cases, rape is committed by someone the victim knows or is acquainted with.

WTF

Why Teens Fail...

Societal views are changing in regard to rape and date rape scenarios. Various states may be more ahead of or behind other states in their attitudes and thus their legislation as it relates to sexual assault.

What To Fix...

Learn what the laws are in your state. Find a victim's advocacy group in your state that can help you if you are struggling with a date rape incident. Resources are available.

Why Teens Fail...

Teen boys and teen girls still have wildly varying views on appropriate initiation of sexual contact. Myths are often perpetuated and negative stereotypes reinforced by popular media, movies, and TV shows.

What To Fix...

Parents should talk to their sons about appropriate and respectful dating boundaries. They should also teach their daughters the importance of saying "no" with confidence and to avoid mixed messages with verbal language and body language.

Laws across the country have evolved as well. It used to be that in order to be considered a sexual assault, physical resistance was a requirement. Definitions of consent have expanded over the years to provide victims with more rights.

Acquaintance or date rape is still a relatively controversial topic in today's society, with both men and women debating the meaning of consent, and many myths still pervasive. There has always been a disproportionate amount of blaming the victim, claiming that the victim "deserved it" for placing herself in a precarious position or dressing a certain way. Another myth is that if a victim is not severely injured or beat up, then they were not raped. And while females make up the majority of date rape victims, males can be victimized as well. The bottom line is that this type of assault is actually quite pervasive among teenage and college-age boys and girls, men and women, regardless of sexual preference, race, or socioeconomic status.

The effects of date rape can be far reaching. Once the victim has been able to come to terms with what has occurred and is able to define what happened to them as "rape," he/she must decide what to do. While the vast majority of victims disclose the assault to at least one person close to them, very few actually report the crime to police, and even fewer choose to aid in prosecution. Some victims may fear the emotional trauma of reliving or retelling the event to police, counselors, prosecutors, or a jury. There is a lot of disbelief, guilt, and self-blame associated with any sexual assault. When the perpetrator is someone the victim knows, trusts, or possibly loves, everything is magnified. For many it is inconceivable that an acquaintance would rape them. Victims can suffer from varying levels of fear, depression, anxiety, adversity in relationships, and difficulty in trying to regain a sense of normalcy in their lives. Victims are at risk of abusing alcohol and drugs and of contemplating suicide. The extent of all of these consequences depends on the individual, their coping style, their personal support network, and any mental health assistance received.

Date rape is becoming more prevalent in the younger generation. More than anything, teenagers want to fit in and are willing to do or try just about anything to feel validated by their peers. Both boys and girls take risks they would not normally take, or that their parents would never think they would take, simply to impress their peers or a member of the opposite sex. This age group is also most likely not willing to speak up in defense of themselves or others for fear of humiliation or being socially ostracized.

In today's society, adolescents are being exposed to sexuality at a very young age. By the time they reach high school they can have become desensitized, and sometimes when they are exposed to unwanted kissing, hugging, genital contact, and sex, they don't know or understand that they have been victimized.

> ## Why Teens Fail...
> *Teens are exposed to sexuality without appropriate boundaries through pop culture and their peers, leading to significantly high percentages of sexual victimization. Often, victims don't realize they are the victims of a crime.*

One out of every six American women has been the victim of an attempted or completed rape in her lifetime (14.8 percent completed rape; 2.8 percent attempted rape).

(National Institute of Justice & Centers for Disease Control & Prevention. *Prevalence, Incidence and Consequences of Violence Against Women Survey.* 1998.)

> ## What To Fix...
> *Find a current news story from the Internet or other source about date rape that you can read and discuss with your teen to identify your family values, attitudes, and beliefs about appropriate sexual contact.*

About **3 percent of American men** — or **1 in 33** — have experienced an attempted or completed rape in their lifetime.

(National Institute of Justice & Centers for Disease Control & Prevention. *Prevalence, Incidence and Consequences of Violence Against Women Survey.* 1998.)

Ninety-three percent of juvenile sexual assault victims know their attacker.

- 34.2 percent of attackers were family members.

- 58.7 percent were acquaintances.

- Only 7 percent of the perpetrators were strangers to the victim.

(US Bureau of Justice Statistics. *2000 Sexual Assaults of Young Children as Reported to Law Enforcement.* 2000.)

As you can see from the statistics above, the idea that date or acquaintance rape is not relevant, is a thing of the past, or doesn't happen in your town or city is incorrect.

Brie's Story

Brie was a troubled young fourteen-year-old girl. She lived with her mom in an apartment after having recently moved to a new state and city. Brie struggled with depression and a low self-image. She was a victim of child molestation and turned to alcohol and drugs to drown out the pain she did not know how to process. Brie had just gotten out of a rehab program and was hoping this time it would work.

One spring evening she was walking in her apartment complex and met a boy. He told her his name, but later she could not seem to remember it. He was older; he told her he was twenty-one. He was nice, funny, and easy to talk to. Brie had seen him in the complex before and he told her he was staying with his aunt. The boy asked her if she wanted to hang out. Brie was having a particularly bad day because the person who had molested her had sent her a message on MySpace that morning. Brie took him up on his offer to hang out and escape.

Brie admitted she drank most of the large bottle of liquor the boy provided her. She thought she was safe with "a friend." Before long, Brie was very intoxicated. She had trouble walking and talking. Then she found herself being pressed up against a car in the parking lot as this "friend" was trying to kiss her and touch her body. When Brie tried to push him off and walk away, she tripped and fell on the ground. The boy was right there to help her up, and because of her condition he was easily able to get her into his apartment and onto a bed.

Most likely due to the alcohol, Brie's memories are full of black holes. She remembers repeatedly saying, "No. Stop. Please don't do this." He didn't listen. Part of what she can remember is the boy having intercourse with her, anal sex, and being forced to perform oral sex on him. Her next full memory is lying naked on a mattress with the boy having just walked to the bathroom. Brie got up, grabbed her clothes, and ran. Getting dressed outside, she took off for her apartment where she realized it was four in the morning. Where had the time gone?

After showering because she felt so dirty, she fell into bed until later that morning when her mother woke her up. Brie was so scared of what her mom would say, she let her mother go off to work without telling her anything. Was this her fault? She should never have gotten that drunk. Did the boy think she was flirting with him? Why didn't she fight harder? Scream louder? Why did stuff like this always happen to her? By the time her mom got home from work, Brie could not hold it in anymore and broke down. Her mom immediately brought her to the hospital and the police were contacted.

However, Brie would not see any "justice" in the criminal court system. She did not know her rapist's name. She was too intoxicated to remember exactly where she had been. The complex was big, full of apartments that looked exactly the same. Every apartment she pointed out to the police belonged to families and no one knew who Brie had described. Brie truly had no idea where she had been attacked or who had attacked her. She was left to pick up the pieces all over again.

What happened to Brie is happening to teenagers and young adults all over the country. Could she have made better choices that night? Choices that would have completely changed what happened to her? Absolutely. But when she said NO, she meant NO, and that boy in the complex is ultimately responsible for raping Brie that spring night. The preteen and teen population is very vulnerable to outside influences. As parents, it is our duty to ensure that our children grow to be teenagers, young adults, and adults. We should never be done helping, teaching, guiding, and ultimately protecting them.

Abby's Story

> **Why Teens Fail...**
>
> *Victims often feel guilt and shame after an unwanted sexual encounter, even if they tried to resist or were overpowered.*

> **What To Fix...**
>
> *Victims should understand that there are various tactics to surviving a rape encounter. Most importantly, if they are still alive after an encounter, they should feel that they made the right choice.*

Abby was a beautiful, vivacious thirteen-year-old girl in eighth grade. She loved to play soccer and hang out with her friends. It was summer and Abby had made a new friend. Her parents were going on a weekend camping trip and agreed to let Abby stay home and spend the weekend at her new friend's house. Once her parents were gone, Abby was convinced by her new friend to go back to Abby's house and throw a little party. Abby wanted to fit in. She really liked her new friend. Does this sound too stereotypical to be true so far? It isn't. This too is a true story.

Mike was invited to the party and showed up with alcohol and something Abby had never heard of before, "Spice." It was like tobacco and it was peach-flavored. (Spice is a synthetic marijuana that is smoked, causing a very intense high similar to marijuana. It is now an outlawed substance in many jurisdictions.) They told her everybody was smoking it. Mike was twenty. Abby thought he liked her friend and that was why he was there. Throughout the night Abby drank vodka and beer and eventually passed out in bed. Early in the morning as everyone was asleep, Mike came into Abby's room. He crawled into bed with her and told her he really liked her. He thought she was pretty and funny and offered her some Spice. She smoked some with Mike. He thought she was pretty! He liked *her*, not her friend! On top of the alcohol she had drunk for the first time, the Spice made her feel very funny, foggy, "out of it."

Mike kissed Abby. It was her first kiss and it felt nice. He then started to touch her body and took off her clothes. Abby did not want to do anything more than kiss, but she didn't know what to say or do. Mike liked her and she did not want him to think she was a little girl! Abby didn't say anything as Mike put on a condom. She was so scared she seemed to freeze. She couldn't say no or push him off. He would laugh at her. At least he was not being mean or hurting her, she told herself. This was not how she thought her first time would be. Abby faded off to sleep with hazy memories of what had just happened.

Why Teens Fail...

Alcohol or illegal drug consumption is a common element to many teen date rape encounters. Victims with impaired judgment or poor physical reaction time make easier targets for sexual predators.

What To Fix...

Teens need to understand that drug and alcohol use leads to a multitude of other risky behaviors, not the least of which is an unwanted sexual encounter. It's easier to say "no" to sex if you already said "no" to impairment.

WTF

Abby's mom was suspicious when they returned home from their camping trip. Something was not right with Abby. And was that a hickey on her neck? When she looked on Abby's phone, she saw text messages. Following her instinct, she began texting with Mike as Abby and found that unfortunately her instinct was right. She went straight to the police.

When interviewed by the police detectives, Mike admitted to the sexual encounter. This wasn't his first encounter with a much younger girl. It seemed he liked to meet girls who were under fifteen. He didn't know why, but he "got along with them so well." Abby just happened to be the first girl who had reported it to police.

Mike eventually pled guilty to lesser charges and spent a total of two years in jail. He will also have to register as a sex offender for the rest of his life. The choices Mike made that night will follow him forever as he has to tell every employer and register every time he moves as a sex offender.

There were choices Abby made that weekend that forever changed her life. She is responsible for making those decisions to break her parents' trust, go back to her house, and throw a party.

Madison's Story

Madison was a seventeen-year-old girl who came from a close-knit religious family. She was homeschooled, and the entire family had been taking karate lessons for years at the same studio. When Madison turned seventeen, she got her license, a car, and a job at the karate studio. She knew everyone there and it was a comfortable place. She had been attending classes there since she was twelve. Madison had a boyfriend, but they had not gone any further than kissing.

At the studio was a karate instructor she had known for years. Noah was a mentor, a first-degree black belt, and thirty-one years old. Madison respected Noah. He had always been very attentive to her, complimented her, and flirted with her, and she looked up to him. She "thought we were friends."

Why Teens Fail...

In most cases, the sexual predator is not a stranger. Predators often gravitate toward positions of influence and trust within the family or the community.

What To Fix...

Be cautious about mentors who try to be alone with teens. Most reputable organizations strive to keep adult mentors in pairs to protect the leaders and the youth.

WTF

Madison thought it a little strange, but Noah began to text her here and there, and then it became more frequent. The topics were first about work, but eventually they became more vulgar and sexual in nature. He told her things he had done sexually and wanted to know what she had done. Noah would ask questions about her boyfriend and give her advice. She thought he was just being a friend.

One night Noah called and asked Madison to stop by the studio to help set up for an event. She had been to the movies with a friend and stopped by on her way home. It was well past 10:00 p.m. and they were alone. Noah told Madison she looked a little sad, and she confided about a fight she had had with her boyfriend earlier that day. Her boyfriend had been pressuring her to have sex and she did not want to go that far. Madison always wore a purity ring pledging her virginity until marriage, and this had been a point of contention with her boyfriend. Noah told Madison that it looked like she needed a hug and gave her a big hug that made her feel good. He then bent down and started kissing her on the lips. Madison was part scared, part thrilled. Noah was a good-looking man whom she looked up to. She kissed him back.

Noah then swept Madison up off her feet and carried her to the leather couch in the office. Madison did not know what to do. He told her how beautiful she was and how she was so easy to talk to. Noah seemed to move smoothly and while the kissing was okay, her jeans were quickly down and his hand was touching her body. She did not know what to do. This was farther than she had ever gone before, or wanted to go. Noah was touching himself too. She had never seen that before. Before she understood what was happening, Noah was performing oral sex on Madison. She was "just lying there" and it was "really freakin' awkward." She stopped Noah and told him that this was awkward and that he needed to stop. Noah wanted to know if he had done something wrong. Madison told him this could not happen and he was almost twice her age.

WTF

Noah told Madison that he really liked her and explained why he thought they could be in a relationship.

Why Teens Fail...

Sexual predators often engage in various "grooming" activities to gain the trust of their victims. Grooming activities often include sex talk and introduction of pornographic material.

What To Fix...

Teach your kids that inappropriate sex talk often leads to sexual contact over time. Teach your kids that it is NEVER appropriate to engage in sexual talk with an adult or receive pornographic material from an adult.

Madison kept reminding him of their age difference and that he was an instructor and knew her whole family. She eventually left, but this was not the end of it. For the next several weeks Noah continued to text Madison and wanted to go out, and repeatedly asked for sexual favors and acts. He told her how he could teach her and show her and "talk her through it." However, when she saw him at work, it was never mentioned and he was completely professional. At some point the texts became too much and she told her youth pastor, her parents, and then reported him to her boss at work, and her parents called the police. Noah was fired after he admitted to the sexual contact. Charges in Madison's case were eventually turned down by the county attorney.

In Madison's case, "grooming" was a key component in the process as Noah exposed sexual things to Madison through inappropriate conversations and texts. He made her feel like he was a good listener and that he was a good friend. This type of behavior is a very common tactic and can include gifts and special privileges. Grooming can occur with children, preteens, and teenagers alike. The perpetrators prey upon the weaknesses they find, and in many cases it can be on a financial or material level.

Madison also made some poor decisions, but she also turned around and made some very hard, grownup decisions. She removed herself from a situation after it started and had enough confidence to make it stop and leave. She could have easily fallen into the trap Noah had laid out over months of grooming. Madison also had the courage to eventually report the incident to an adult who could help her.

WTF

Teenage girls need self-esteem more than anything else. It provides them with the ability to stand for what they believe in, what is right, despite how it might make them look to their friends or peers. One key source of self-esteem for a boy or a girl is their parents. Parents play a vital role in developing their child's boundaries, sense of right and wrong, and most of all, self-value and worth. It is not something that happens overnight. This is developed

Why Teens Fail...

Girls (and boys, for that matter) are easier targets for all kinds of crime, including sexual assault, if they have low self-esteem.

What To Fix...

Parents should take special care to build up their daughters' self-esteem in a world where pop media seems to take extra steps to make girls feel inadequate.

over your child's elementary, preteen, and teenage years. Have you built that foundation for your child?

If you are the parent to a boy, your role is equally as important as for parents of girls. Have you taught your son to respect himself and others? Does he understand what it means to be a gentleman? There is never an excuse for violence of any kind toward a girl/woman. Have you told him that consent can be withdrawn at any point in time? And no does not mean yes if you pressure someone long enough? You do not want to be the one responding to a police station after your son is arrested for date rape.

Know who your child is. Know everything about who their friends are. What are they doing and who are they hanging out with? You are their parent, not their best friend. Don't be afraid to parent, to look in their room, on their cell phone and computer. Be involved. Be the person they come to when they are troubled or confused. Be invasive to keep your child safe.

Talk to your child early about sex and sexuality and don't be embarrassed about it. Help them to develop their own sexual boundaries and to hold on to them. Facts and ideals should come from you and not something they heard in the lunchroom at school. Empower your child. Teach your girls to respect themselves and their bodies. Tell them that do not have to remain quiet and polite if they find themselves in a threatening or uncomfortable situation. Teach your boys to respect themselves and girls. Help provide them with the tools to make the right decisions now so that you will not have to help him or her get to the police station or hospital to make a report about an incident that has changed your preteen or teenager's life forever.

Drugs & Alcohol

Drugs can be used by perpetrators when committing sexual assault. Drugs like Rohypnol ("roofies"), gamma hydroxybutyrate (GHB), and ketamine. Drugs like these can easily be mixed in drinks to make

Why Teens Fail...

Some parents are afraid to talk to their kids about sex for a variety of reasons, including awkwardness, shyness, inadequacy, or feelings of hypocrisy.

What To Fix...

Identify your personal values about appropriate sexual contact and make sure that your values are supported by your own behavior. Stress the consequences of specific values, attitudes, and behaviors.

somebody lose consciousness and forget things that transpire. People who have been given these drugs report feeling paralyzed, having fuzzy vision, and experiencing lack of memory. Memories they do have tend to be in flashes. Even worse, mixing these drugs with alcohol can be dangerous and possibly fatal. Drugs such as cocaine, marijuana, and methamphetamines can also be willingly ingested and leave a person unable to control themselves and/or the circumstances they are in.

Alcohol is more readily available and has become a more acceptable way for perpetrators to render their victim incapacitated. It's much easier to provide alcohol in the form of shots, beer, or hard liquor and encourage overconsumption. This in turn leads victims to self-blame since they willingly consumed the alcohol in many instances.

Educate your preteens and teenagers about the dangers of the different kinds of drugs and abusing alcohol. Encourage your child to stay sober, alert, and mindful of what is going on around them.

Warning Signs

Unfortunately, as parents we may do everything in our power to prepare our children for making good choices and staying out of danger, but sometimes it is not enough. If you notice something is not right with your son or daughter, don't ignore it. Some things to look out for can include but are not limited to:

Acting abnormally irritable, moody, or cranky. Do they seem angry, frightened, or confused? Do they seem anxious, nervous, or afraid to be alone? Have they withdrawn from family, friends, or school? Is there a change in their everyday habits such as eating or sleeping? If any behaviors seem concerning to you, reach out to your child and let them know that you are there for them. If your child does not respond to your reaching out, contact another adult your child may be close to, or a professional may need to provide assistance. Do whatever it takes to get to the bottom of why your child is displaying these changes.

Why Teens Fail...

Sexual assault is a serious crime and the criminal justice system has rigorous standards when it comes to proving a sexual assault has occurred. Often, cases are dismissed due to lack of evidence.

What To Fix...

If you or a loved one is believed to be the victim of sexual assault, seek medical and police assistance within twenty-four hours if possible. Don't shower or change clothes before receiving medical attention.

WTF

Adults have difficulties processing and dealing to the aftermath of a date rape, and it can be much more dramatic for a teenager who does not have the ability to process what has happened. Remember above all else, nobody invites sexual assault, and nobody deserves to be attacked, demeaned, or forced to do something they do not want to do.

CHAPTER 8
PLAY IT SAFE
BY LAURA LATHAM, SELF-DEFENSE EXPERT

On every playground across the world, boys insult other boys with the insult of all insults: "You fight like a girl!" What I didn't learn until my adulthood is that for a girl, fighting like a girl can be the difference between life and death. I am not talking about a playground fistfight between two boys over a cheap shot on the basketball court at recess. No, not even close. When a man fights a woman, it is serious and the stakes are high. I am talking about you on your back (we will discuss later what pre-indicators you may have missed to be in this position, but right now it doesn't matter), and the predator has you pinned to the ground. He is in between your legs and he is going to rape you. Will you live through the assault? It is completely up to him...or is it? You have one life and you better fight for it, but you must fight *smart* and fight like Girls on Guard ™!

WTF

Girls on Guard is a self-defense strategy for teenage girls and women. When I use the word "fight," I am not talking about mutual combat. The word fight in this case means using force to escape. This is a worst case scenario and you are under assault; you are being attacked. It is too late to run or try to talk your way out of the assault, and the only option you have left is to fight. We need to consider that bad things happen to good people for no reason; no one is immune. It can happen to you, moms, and it can happen to your daughters.

When it comes to teen sexual abuse, the problem is more common than one would think. In most teen sexual abuse assaults, the victims know their abuser. Alcohol and drugs also can play a big role in the assault. In this chapter I am addressing more of an attack by a stranger, as acquaintance rape is being covered in chapter seven. Although rare, stranger attacks can happen, and you and your teen need to be armed with the knowledge, skills, and tools to prevent her from being a crime statistic. This chapter is not meant to scare you, this chapter is about reality.

I learned a few hard lessons early in my law enforcement career. I learned first and foremost about the gift of intuition we have been given. I learned the hard way what happens when we rationalize and ignore our intuition. I also learned men are stronger than most women, men know how to fight, and women rely too spray, a key between their fingers—insert your false security measure here). The greatest thing I learned is I had no clue what it felt like to be hit hard by a man, or how ineffective any of the training I had was for this encounter. In the heat of battle is when I realized these things, and it left me physically frozen and totally defenseless. The only reason I am here to write these words is because the man who hated women so much that he refused to let a female police officer arrest him did not choose to kill me.

Why Teens Fail...

Women and children generally have lower density muscle mass than most men. Male attackers are simply stronger than most females and children.

What To Fix...

Women and children need a different defense strategy. It usually does not make sense to fight a man like a man when you cannot match his physical strength. Time to adopt a new tactic!

 **WTF**

If I had not been in that situation, I still would not be able to comprehend what it really means to be attacked by a man. I tried to fight a man like a man, and I got my butt kicked. Women's only chance in a fight against a man is to fight like a Girls on Guard.

How I Got My Butt Kicked

I was twenty-three years old and had recently completed my police field training with no problems, and I was finally on my own. I had just checked in for my shift and was heading toward my assigned area of town. I was dispatched a "silent panic alarm" call coming from the inside of a residence. This was a two-officer type of call, but I immediately cancelled my back-up unit because I felt I could handle this call alone, since I had actually been to this particular residence several times for false "motion detector" alarms. The home's residents, a husband, wife, and small child, had cats that would set off the motion detector. Every time I had previously responded to the house alarm, investigation revealed the motion detector was set off by their cats.

On my way to the house it dawned on me that in the past all the false alarms had been motion detector alarms. This call was a silent panic alarm. I even pulled up the history of all the prior calls at this house to confirm I was correct. I remember telling myself that it was probably dispatched wrong and was the usual false motion detector alarm. Darn cats!

As I pulled up to the house, I began to have a bad feeling. As I got out of my patrol car and started walking to the door, I could feel the hair on the back of my neck stand up. I can't describe the feeling, although I remember ignoring whatever my body was telling me.

I knocked on the door and the male homeowner opened it. I greeted him by name and said, "It's me again." That was the instant I knew something was wrong. He had always been friendly to me in the past, but this time was different. He only opened the door about a foot and he had a frozen stare. I remember thinking that there was probably someone standing behind him with a gun to his head. I spoke in to my radio using the shoulder microphone attached to my collar, requesting a second unit respond to my location. I asked him if everything was okay. He responded in an unusual monotone voice, "Everything is just fine." I noticed his right hand was bloody and wrapped in a paper towel. I asked if his wife and son were home and he said they were in the back of the house. I asked if I could see them and he replied, "Not until I see a warrant!" He then attempted to shut the door, but I was able to get my foot in the doorway and shouldered the door open. I was now in his house standing face to face with him. He was 6' 4" and weighed about 250 pounds. As it turned out, he was drunk. He started going

Why Teens Fail...

We have a dangerous tendency to rationalize away our intuition. All too often we tell ourselves everything is fine, when our so-called sixth sense is screaming otherwise.

What To Fix...

Our five senses are picking up clues to our environment on both a conscious and a subconscious level. Just because you cannot consciously articulate a danger does not mean that it does not exist. Trust your instincts!

crazy and was screaming and cursing at me, but all I could think to myself was, "Why are you doing this? I am here to help you." My mind was completely frozen; I had never mentally prepared to be attacked by someone, let alone a man. In my world, men did not hit women. In the police academy we had to fight as part of our training, but my partner was always a female. I was not physically prepared for this fight either.

He grabbed me by the left wrist and I tried to break his grasp, but I was no match for his strength. I remember making a fist with my right hand and cocking my arm back to punch him. Guess what he did? The exact same thing! I was smart enough to know that if I punched him he was going to punch me back ten times harder.

So instead I reached for my pepper spray that was on my gun belt around my waist (not in the bottom of a purse where most women keep it, which would have been impossible to get to). For those of you who carry pepper spray, I have a question for you. How many of you have been sprayed directly in the face with it? If you haven't, you need to so you will know how it affects you. I am one of the few who has a very bad reaction to pepper spray (most people it really does not affect). I immediately feel like I am suffocating and can't breathe. The man who was still gripping my wrist was wearing glasses. I was worried that if I sprayed the stream of pepper spray at him, it would bounce off his glasses and hit me in the face. He tried to take my pepper spray from me, so I threw it behind his couch. I tried to get back on my radio to yell for immediate help, but then he grabbed my right wrist.

WTF

He now had me by both wrists and I tried to free my arms with the wrist-lock escapes I had learned in the police academy. I couldn't remember if I was supposed to go up and over or down and under. I tried both. Neither worked, his grip was so strong. I then got the brilliant idea to knee him in the groin. What a joke! First of all the groin is not a big target (pause for laughs), and from the age of two or three, boys learn instinctively to go to great lengths to protect the groin. I still attempted a knee strike to the

Why Teens Fail...

Many people, including police officers, become complacent and put too much faith in a particular defense tool. This is called overdependence and can result in misuse of an otherwise useful weapon.

What To Fix...

Don't rely on pepper spray or mace to protect you from a dedicated attacker, especially when your tool of choice is not accessible. You need to form a Plan B. More on this to follow...

groin that I had practiced hundreds of times in the police academy. Guess what? He blocked it.

By now he had lifted me off the ground and I was being slammed into the wall. I still honestly could not understand what was happening and why he was doing this to me. Remember, I was there to help him! I had a radio, a baton, and a gun all attached to my waist and could not reach any of them. I remembered almost laughing to myself about my career choice and thinking that I had no business being a police officer. I was no match for him. His wife then appeared from the back of the house and started screaming at me, too. I later learned he had been beating her up and she was the one who had triggered the silent panic alarm to call the police for help.

After what seemed like forever, the first two officers arrived. I have to admit I felt a little better when the first officer (a big, tough guy) got knocked on his butt by the man who had assaulted me. It took a few officers to finally get this man into handcuffs. As it turned out he actually said he didn't care if he was going to jail, but no woman was going to be the one to arrest him.

Obviously this is a different situation than what you may face one day. I went to my attacker as a police officer doing my job; I was being paid not to run away. While the details of most assault victims' experiences will differ from case to case, here are a few principles every woman should take away from my experience.

First of all, from the very beginning I did not trust my intuition. I knew immediately that something about this call was wrong, but I rationalized it and ignored my feelings. I had the luxury of having a radio and was able to call for help prior to things getting really ugly; you won't have a radio connected to police dispatch attached to your collar if you are attacked. Once things got ugly, he kept me from getting on my radio or being able to reach the tools I was wearing around my waist and had trained with daily. Where do you carry your self-defense tools? Probably not around your waist, and I doubt you practice pulling them out quickly. You need to accept the fact right now that you will be alone and you must be ready and able to save yourself empty-handed.

Why Teens Fail...

Many self-defense instructors teach women and children to aim a blow at the groin of a male attacker to fend him off. This strategy usually fails for a number of reasons.

What To Fix...

If your counterattack is blocked and the "soft target" is well defended, you need a strategy that will overcome your attacker's superior physical strength... a strategy like Girls On Guard (more on this later).

Next, the most important lesson I learned in this attack was I am not as strong or violent as a man. I can't fight a man like a man fights by standing on my feet. I made it through the next fifteen years just fine. Sure, I had my share of fights, but trusting my intuition kept me out of several more, I'm sure of it.

Third, I learned that when things start to go bad, I need to be the one to strike first. I don't freeze and ask myself, "Why is this happening to me?" I also have a different confidence about me that tells people not to even try and mess with me, something I definitely did not have in my first encounter.

The man who attacked me had personal feelings toward women that are common characteristics of men who prey on women. Yes, I am a woman, smaller and weaker than most men. The predator wants to prey on what he thinks are my vulnerabilities. He wants to punch me, slam me into the wall, and maybe even kill me. He wants me to pay for all the women who did him wrong, or for the fact his mother did not love him. The predator doesn't know me or care to know me. He wants to leave me so psychologically damaged that I will never be sure of myself again, that I will never have a normal, happy life. The predator doesn't care that I am a mom because he has sick urges and he needs a victim. He needs a woman to exert power and control over and he doesn't care who it is. But you need to care, and your daughters needs to care. Then, if you are ever attacked, you will not be a victim; you will be a survivor.

WTF

Why Teens Fail...

Many attackers are empowered by drugs or alcohol which in some cases may actually enhance their strength or endurance and will certainly give them the illusion that they are stronger and more invulnerable than they actually are.

What To Fix...

Be aware of the potential for "chemically enhanced" courage on the part of the attacker. Be prepared to exploit his slower reflexes and reaction time.

The Difference between Survivors and Victims

If you decide now that you are going to fight back, you have just increased your chance of survival by 50 percent. What that means is by fighting back, you double your chance of survival. A US Department of Justice study revealed that half of all attackers will break off their attack if the woman simply indicates she is willing to resist. *Half of the attackers!* The next pages will address what to do regarding the other half of attackers who continue the attack. That same Department of Justice study showed that women who resist are not injured any more than women who don't resist, and 96 percent of injuries to women who resist are only cuts and scrapes!

Another call I responded to as a police officer was an attempted rape in an apartment near a college campus. I was the first officer to arrive and will never forget how badly the survivor (never victim) was shaking. Prior to my arrival the attacker had run off, but I could still sense his smell in her bedroom. She had been sleeping and had left the front door unlocked for her roommate. She awoke to a knife pressed against her throat. She immediately kicked and screamed and that is when the predator left. Her throat did get cut and she needed three sutures. While I was at the hospital with her, she told me she had taken a self-defense class years earlier, and had made up her mind back then that she was going to fight if she was ever attacked. She also told me that when she felt the knife against her throat she didn't even have to think about what she was going to do; she just reacted.

Every criminal has two fears: the fear of getting caught, and the fear of getting hurt. The predator has the advantage because he has a plan. In his mind he has gone over how the crime will go down; this attack is far more mental than physical. He is going to use the compliant fear factor; he wants you to comply through fear. The predator thinks he has the advantage. Little does he know the advantage lies with you: he is going to have to make a major adjustment, because you knew this was coming. You are going to sensory-deprive him! If he tells you not to scream, SCREAM YOUR HEAD OFF! Ruin his plan. The predator may freeze or panic and run away. Don't do what he says and hope he won't hurt you. Hope alone is not a strategy!

WTF ➤

> ## Why Teens Fail...
>
> *Violent male attackers are seeking submissive women who will not fight back. They plan on the submissive nature of the victim to execute their attack.*

> ## What To Fix...
>
> *Statistically, half of the women who fight back against their attackers cause the attacker to break off his assault. Studies indicate that women who fight back are not significantly more injured than those victims who submit.*

What if the predator has a gun? Although rape and sexual assaults are the least likely violent crime to involve a weapon, you have an 85 percent chance of survival after being shot with a handgun if you get to a hospital within forty minutes! Think about Gabrielle Giffords, the Arizona congresswomen who was shot point-blank in the head and survived. Do *not* allow yourself to be taken to a secondary crime scene. Every police officer will agree on this one—the second location is where the really awful things happen. It has been estimated that 95 percent of victims taken to a second location will die, and it will be on the predator's terms. I would rather die in the parking lot of a mall than into his car and die after days of torture. If I am foolish enough to get in that car, maybe years later hikers will find my bones in the desert which will give my family some closure, or maybe my bones will never be found and my family will never know for sure. Submitting has consequences; it places you under his control.

Why Teens Fail...

A common characteristic of many victims is that they never saw the attack coming, and were thus unprepared to deal with the encounter.

Develop Your Killer Instinct

That killer instinct—we all have it, but we all control it differently. Are you the one at the haunted house who screams and hides when someone jumps out, or are you in their face ready to punch them? That will tell you how you handle your killer instinct. With a predator, the worst thing you can do is show fear. Panic causes hesitation, and the first four to five seconds are most critical. Everyone has about a second and a half of reaction time for their brain to process the fact that some guy just grabbed them from behind and is dragging them into an alley.

What To Fix...

Play the "what if" game with yourself when you are in a vulnerable situation. Would I run? Scream? What would I say? Do I have any weapons close at hand? Do I have a plan? If not, GET ONE!

If you predetermine the outcome, you are so much ahead! That means going over in your mind different scenarios before they happen. To always think about being attacked doesn't make you paranoid, it makes you *prepared!* (To think about being attacked by vampires, that makes you paranoid.) You need to have a heightened sense of alertness at all times as to how you look at people and situations. You will then be able to notice the warning signs and signals when something is not right. Play the "what if" game with yourself all the time. You should be thinking what you would do if a predator came through your front door this very moment. What if a predator were hiding in the bushes next to your car? What would you do? Playing the what-if game today can make the difference between life and death tomorrow. Little does the predator know that you have seen him coming, and you have a plan. You have mentally prepared for this day.

Prepare for the Fight of Your Life

How many of you remember "stop, drop, and roll"? How many of you have caught on fire? That is what Girls on Guard is like. The chances of a violent stranger attack are slim, but just like you could catch on fire, this is a worst case scenario. How many of you have taken a self-defense class before?

Every class I have ever taken or taught up until now says to stay on your feet and fight like a man. As I have already told you from my experience, it does not work! Girls On Guard is not a martial arts program. Rape is a crime of violence. When a man is attacked, the predator wants his property or his life. When a woman is attacked, the predator wants her property, her body, her life, or all three.

No other self-defense program really addresses sexual assaults. They teach you to poke him in the eye, kick him in the groin, palm strike him in the nose—that is a fight! This program will not teach you how to fight. The purpose of this program is to teach you how to *escape*. No wrist locks, nothing to remember! I saw a martial artist on TV showing women how they can successfully fight off an attacker with a tube of lipstick. Really?

How about this advice? I read in a self-defense book about how to defend against a punch or kick: "see it coming, then move out of the way." Wow, I'm not even sure how to respond to that one! Attacks are fast, hard, and violent. Unfortunately, you may not see it coming.

Step One: Run

What is the strongest part of a woman's body? Her legs! In a rape scenario the predator's ultimate goal is to get you on the ground...*to rape you!* As soon as you sense you're in danger, you need to run to a safe place. A safe place is anywhere there are people.

Why Teens Fail...

As many as 95 percent of victims who submit to their attackers and are taken to a secondary crime scene are ultimately killed by their attackers.

What To Fix...

Never submit to being taken to a secondary crime scene. Decide now that you will fight tooth and nail in order to avoid being taken to another location. You have an 85 percent chance of surviving a gunshot wound if you get to a hospital fast

Step two: Temper Tantrum

If you are not able to run and get away, the moment the predator grabs you, *have a self-defense temper tantrum!* Fall out of his grip, go to the ground, and kick, kick, kick! Scream, "911!" You are not going to scream "fire" as many self-defense instructors teach; when you try to do the opposite of what comes naturally, you get into trouble. When you're under stress and your heart rate increases, you unknowingly hold your breath, which can cause you to pass out. You need to scream, not only to attract attention while now sensory-depriving the predator, but you also hit and kick harder when you are screaming. Think of a martial artist breaking a brick—it is not done in silence. He or she yells, "Kiai!"

Under stress you lose your fine motor skills. You won't be able to make your index finger work to even deploy pepper spray (which is probably expired and at the bottom of your purse, anyway). Under stress you will only have use of your gross motor skills. The good news is that when your fine motor skills fail, your gross motor skills step up. You will hit and kick harder and run faster than ever. Think of people who lift cars off loved ones in times of extreme stress. They could never do that in a natural state.

WTF

> **Why Teens Fail...**
>
> *Under stress, most people untrained in martial arts lose all fine motor skills that are required for complex defensive tactics (joint locks, pressure points, eye-gouges, etc.).*

> **What To Fix...**
>
> *With much less training, we can utilize the stress of an attack to maximize our gross motor skills (speed and strength) to fend off an attacker. G.O.G. incorporates this philosophy.*

Why Girls on Guard Works

Defend University is a research and development group dedicated to the exploration of leading-edge techniques. Defend University was founded by Brad Parker and Steve Kardian, who have been amazing friends and mentors to me and are also experts in the field of self-defense. With their combined experience, they developed a program that gives women the best chance of effectively defending themselves from sexual assaults. Girls On Guard teaches women to use their strongest weapons, legs, against a man's weakest and most vulnerable points: his knees, groin, and face, all the way up his centerline from his knees to his nose. Women can strengthen their legs, but a man's primary targets can't be strengthened. Girls On Guard does not rely on pain compliance, because over 60 percent of all felons are on some sort of intoxicant at the time of the crime. This program was designed by survivors of sexual assaults; Brad and Steve studied real life sexual assaults to develop effective, gross-body responses applied in a realistic role-playing environment with regular, non–martial arts women. This program was not designed by military specialists or black belts in the martial arts, but by women, for women. With Girls On Guard, women are not given a lot of options, because the more options you have the more time it takes you to choose (Hicks Law).

In Girls On Guard, the ground is your friend. Immediately sit on the ground—think hips to heels—and then use your strongest weapons (legs, hips, and trunk muscles) against his weakest, most vulnerable targets. Your legs are a barrier and will always be longer than his arms, so he can't reach you to hit or cho **WTF**

Remember, your main goal is not necessarily to hurt him…you are trying to get away! If you happen to rupture a testicle, whoops! Fight to the goal, and the goal is to escape. What do you think is a woman's worst fear? Being raped and murdered by a man. Time and time again this is the answer I am given when I ask a woman that question.

Rapists come in all shapes and sizes, and it is impossible to identify who among us is a predator. It is impossible to avoid every opportunity that a rapist may take to attack you, and there is never any guarantee against an attack. It is also impossible to determine who will be chosen by the predator, but it is possible to reduce the odds of being attacked. Teenage girls can be a perfect target for a predator due to the fact they are naïve, trusting, and inexperienced. Ninety percent of survivors know their attacker and most cases involve alcohol.

Take a Girls on Guard class with your daughter. You will actually learn in a training environment while being coached by an instructor in what it feels like to be attacked by a man (wearing a padded suit—not for your safety, for his). Although a predator will attack harder and faster and with more surprise, it shouldn't be a complete

Why Teens Fail...

Ground fighting is a highly specialized martial art that requires a great deal of training in most cases. Most male attackers know that their victims are at a disadvantage on the ground when it comes to traditional fighting techniques.

What To Fix...

G.O.G. changes this traditional point of view so that being on the ground becomes an advantage to the victim. You can learn how to turn the tables on an attacker by going to the ground, even if he is bigger and stronger.

surprise if this ever happens to you in the "real world." A shock, yes, but not a surprise; you have trained for this moment. You are mentally prepared. Just having that confidence about you will make a predator think twice about targeting you.

The Secret Weapon: Confidence

I read a study of convicted rapists who all said they chose their victims by *how they walked!* Confidence is your secret weapon. Confidence is the key to staying safe. I don't care if you have to "fake it to make it," but you have to walk and stand with confidence.

Remember, what is the number one fear of a predator? The fear of getting caught. What is his number two fear? The fear of getting hurt. The predator is looking for an easy target, one who will comply and not fight back. This is what self-defense experts call a soft target. A soft target is a person who is thinking about what she will be doing in an hour, not what she is doing *right now*. Get off your cell phone, stop texting or listening to your iPod. Make eye contact with people. Let them know "I SEE YOU," and not only that, give a total mad-dogging message saying, "I see you; I see you well and clear. I will remember you. I will identify you and could pick you out of a police lineup if I had to." Mad-dogging is a self-defense technique! The predator does not care who you are, it is irrelevant. If you are a hard target, the predator can always find a soft target elsewhere. Remember, he does not want to get caught or hurt. Humans, even predators, are predictable. If someone knows he can't get away with something, he won't even try. For example, seeing a police officer in your rearview mirror will force you to drive the speed limit.

Hone Your Intuition

TRUST YOUR INSTINCTS! Gavin de Becker writes extensively about this in *The Gift of Fear*, a book I recommend all women read. In every society, men are

---

Why Teens Fail...

Attackers are known to search out victims that exhibit body language that is indicative of poor self-esteem and who appear to have low self-confidence.

What To Fix...

If you lack self-confidence, fake it until you make it. Stand tall. Keep your shoulders back. Chin up. Make eye contact. Walk with intent. Your body language is your first line of defense against a would-be attacker.

more violent than women. So while God was giving men big muscles, he forgot about us! I think God made up for this by giving women the gift of intuition. The problem is we *ignore* it! When we ignore our intuition, we are nothing more than a man with no muscles! What happens when deer hear a twig snap in the woods? They run! Deer don't question what they just heard, they don't stand there and try to justify and rationalize why the twig snapped. Yet women, sensing something is wrong, don't listen.

How many of you have "Creepdar"? The Urban Dictionary defines this as the ability to discern the creepiness of another person. You know that feeling when, for whatever reason, a guy just creeps you out? Most of us have been in an elevator or waiting at a crosswalk for the light to change when a man stands next to you and gets too close. A nice guy senses that you're uncomfortable, is embarrassed that he got too close and made you feel uncomfortable, and he steps away. *The creep doesn't move.* Let the creep know that you know he is a creep, and get off on the next floor or let him cross the street and you wait for the next light. If you think the guy is a creep, he probably is! Several rape survivors said they ignored their gut feelings because they didn't want to be rude! I am giving you permission, ladies: *Be rude!* Your momentary rudeness will not make a nice guy turn violent. Remember, your safety first...his feelings last.

WTF

Trust yourself that you are right, not him to prove your instincts were right! The most frustrating part about trusting your instincts is you won't ever know if your instincts were right; the only confirmation you will have is when he is raping and killing you. Then you will know that your instincts were right.

There are two basic types of strategies that a predator can use: charm and blitz. The blitz strategy is when the predator uses speed, power, and environment to take control. Once again, this is where being a hard target will come into play. This type of predator will choose someone who appears to him as a soft target, someone who appears to not be paying attention, is unaware of her surroundings and looks afraid, and could be easily intimidated and overtaken. The charm strategy is when the

Why Teens Fail...

Women and teens are sometimes afraid to be rude to strangers. When approached by a stranger, many would-be victims are afraid to say, "Stop! Don't come any closer!" because they don't want to offend a would-be attacker!

What To Fix...

Say: STOP! DON'T COME ANY CLOSER!

A well-meaning stranger will realize they have crossed your boundaries and back off. An attacker will continue to advance, giving you crucial advanced warning.

predator may approach you in a group, but he will be there alone and his goal will be to separate you from your friends and take you to someplace private. The charm predator will use "interview" techniques on you, without your even knowing, to get information about you—who you came with, where you live, what type of car you drive. This gives him more than enough information to plan an attack. When someone you don't know is being nice to you, ask yourself why? Is your creepdar going off? If it is, you need to listen to it. The charmer-predator will not take no for an answer and will insist on buying you a drink or walking you to your car. Verbal de-escalation is ineffective with either type of predator. With a charm predator, a loud, aggressive "I said NO! Back off!" will usually work. This will work because it will draw attention, which is the last thing a predator wants.

Stranger attacks are very rare, but they do happen. Whenever possible, avoid being alone or isolated with a stranger; don't walk alone at night. Go out as a group, leave as a group! Never, ever let yourself be taken to a second crime scene. Trust your instincts. Don't ignore a stranger; let him know you see him. If you sense he is a creep, go with your gut feelings. Have a readiness plan of attack. Explore the "what ifs." Go over in your mind what you're going to do if someone tries to break into your house or jumps in your car while you're stopped at a red light.

Trying to decide what you're going to do while under duress is the worst time to make a decision. Each second spent planning how you will react to the predator is another second of damage he is inflicting on you. That damage will decrease your ability to execute your plan. You can be getting killed while attempting to come up with the perfect plan.

Play It Safe

With younger children, both boys and girls, it is ridiculous that we as parents just talk to our children about strangers. Did you talk to your kids about swimming and

Why Teens Fail...

Victims are usually alone when attacked. Predators seek out easy targets. A lone person is a much easier target than a group of two or three.

What To Fix...

There is safety in numbers. Stay with a friend when walking through potentially dangerous areas, especially at night. Two friends might be even better than one friend!

then throw them in the swimming pool? No, you gave them swimming lessons.

Many parents put their kids in karate for self-defense training. I think any type of martial arts training is good for kids, as it teaches them discipline and is great exercise. But I do not think martial arts are effective for self-defense other than giving kids confidence. As with women, the key to kids' staying safe is confidence. Confident kids are less likely to get bullied, confident kids are less likely to get abducted, and confident women are less likely to get raped.

Thankfully, kidnapping by strangers is so rare I can cover this topic in a few paragraphs. First and foremost, we as parents are failing our children, as *we* are the first line of defense for our children. I can't count how many times I've been in a public place and watched as a mother picked up her purse and went into the bathroom while leaving her child in the play area alone!

I have seen it the other way around as well: the mother will allow her young son or daughter to go into a public restroom alone while staying at the table or on the park bench (with her purse safely by her side!). Try following this rule: wherever you take your purse, take you child! Although very rare, it can and has happened that children go into a public bathroom alone, only to find a predator waiting inside, or following them in. In one tragic incident in Southern California, the child's aunt was actually outside of the door as a drug user under the influence of psychedelics went inside and slashed the throat of her nine-year-old nephew. He then walked out and acknowledged her as he walked past. Most child abductions occur when children are walking to and from school. You must insist your child walks with someone to school and home every day, or walk with a group, which is even better.

The last detail I was assigned to as a police officer was detective on the US Marshals Violent Criminal Apprehension Team. Our job was to hunt down and find the most violent felons who had been dodging law enforcement officers. We were also tasked with arresting

Why Teens Fail...

Mothers have been observed taking their purse with them into the restroom while leaving their children unattended.

What To Fix...

Follow the Purse Rule of Thumb: if you would not leave your purse unattended, then you probably should not leave your child unattended.

convicted child sexual predators who had either violated the terms of their probation or parole, or who were wanted for failing to register as a sex offender in the county of residence. The entire neighborhood is notified when a registered sex offender has moved into the neighborhood, and there is justifiable cause for concern when that person is living near you and your children. The sex offenders who violate the law and don't register as a sex offender, then move into your neighborhood, are the ones to really be concerned about. At this moment there are currently approximately eight hundred outstanding warrants in Maricopa County for failure to register as a sex offender (Arizona Department of Public Safety Sex Offender Compliance Unit). These criminals are extremely hard to find; they are smarter than most criminals and know how not to leave a paper trail to where they are living. I have arrested several offenders living in nice gated communities, as the gate adds another layer of protection for people who live there, including sex offenders. Once we found one of these criminals and took them into custody, the detective assigned the case had to transport the offender to jail. We were in undercover cars and the fugitive would be seated next to me in the front passenger seat, since there was no cage like in a patrol car (and you would never seat them behind you). Sometimes the ride to the jail could be long, and at times I would talk to sex offenders just to try and understand what was going on in their heads. One in particular explained to me how totally and completely sick he was, and there was no cure. He told me he could be sitting in his house, not even thinking about a child, when a girl or boy would walk past his window. At that point it was like the strongest drug and he could not resist the urge. He was crying when he told me the only way he will ever be able to stop himself is when he is dead. My conversation with him made me realize that not all predators are out looking for a target. For lack of a better phrase, with some offenders it is almost a "crime of opportunity." Do not give the predator an opportunity to harm your child!

Why Teens Fail...

People are too frequently unaware of the registered sex offenders living in or near their neighborhoods.

What To Fix...

Utilize your state's government web page to locate registered sex offenders by your ZIP code. Or you can use a website like www.familywatchdog.us to check for potential bad guys.

WTF

Children need to be told over and over not to go anywhere alone, and parents need to follow that rule too. When I teach a group of children about stranger awareness, all children agree a stranger is "someone they don't know." When I show them a picture of a policeman and ask them if he is a "good" stranger or a "bad" stranger, every child (and the parents too) will agree a policeman is a "good" stranger. I love the blank look on their faces (even the parents) when I ask them what is the police officer's name. If you do not know him, he is a "don't know!" There are not a lot of bad strangers in the world, and the man in the photo probably is a police officer, but if you do not know him he is a "don't know."

We have all told our children not to talk to strangers; we should also be teaching them not to *listen* to strangers. A "good" stranger does not ask a child a question or for help, *ever*. It is okay for a stranger to speak to a child if the parent is present. A child's **biggest weapon is their voice**, and the moment a stranger talks to a child without a parent present, they need to run to a safe place (a safe place is anywhere there are people) while yelling, "STRANGER, STRANGER!" The last thing any predator wants is attention.

> **Why Teens Fail...**
>
> Attackers have a plan that involves not getting caught and not getting hurt. They will look for the easiest target in order to achieve that plan.

> **What To Fix...**
>
> Just carrying yourself in such a way that you no longer look like a soft target will avert most attackers. People who carry themselves with poise develop more confidence; more confident people carry themselves with more poise.

WTF

Lastly, we need to teach our children what to do if a stranger actually grabs them and tries to pull them somewhere, e.g., a car or bathroom. The moment the stranger grabs them, the child needs to throw him- or herself on the ground and have a "self-defense temper tantrum and go CHIHUAHUA CRAZY!" All kids know what a temper tantrum is, and we all know how hard it is to pick up a two-year-old having a tantrum. Can you imagine trying to pick up a ten- year-old child having a tantrum? Children need to use their strongest weapons, **their legs**, to kick, and **their voice**, to scream **"STRANGER, STRANGER, 911!"** The kids love the comparison to the Chihuahua and understand what it means to go "Chihuahua crazy." Most kids have seen the Disney movie *Beverly Hills Chihuahua* and remember the empowerment felt by the Chihuahua who fought off the big bad Doberman pinscher—"We are tiny, but we are mighty," says the Chihuahua.

Why Teens Fail...

Teens are just as much at risk of abduction as toddlers, if not more. This is due in part to the fact that teens put themselves in more dangerous situations.

What To Fix...

Girl On Guard (GOG) classes are designed to teach women and teens tactics that actually work against men. GOG is not a martial arts program. It is a simple strategy with effective tactics to protect your life. Find and take a GOG class.

Sadly, in reality, the stranger is not always who we need to be most afraid of when it comes to protecting our children. Teaching children "stranger danger" must mean that people they know are safe will not harm them, right? Wrong. In the book *Protecting the Gift* by Gavin de Becker (a must-read for parents), the author predicts with near-perfect statistical certainty that *your child will not be kidnapped by a stranger.* It is the people we introduce into our child's lives that we need to worry about.

Children have alarms just like adults do. I call it the "yucky" feeling they get in their tummy. Children need to listen to their feelings and know what to do with them. Teach your child it is okay to say, "NO, I DO NOT LIKE THAT!" to an adult. It is okay to be assertive and defy an adult. It is okay to yell at an adult. Tell your child he or she needs to tell you when someone makes them feel yucky inside. Your child needs to understand that they do not keep secrets from you, and if someone tells them "not to tell," they need to tell. Make sure your child knows with certainty that you are able to protect yourself and your family if someone ever threatens to hurt you if your child tells on them.

Get your child self-defense lessons that teach kids realistic ways to defend themselves. I just don't believe that pinching a predator's arm or stomping on his foot will be successful in breaking off an attack.

Kids' throwing themselves on the ground is not only effective, it is natural! Finally, role play with your children at home. Make a game out of it; pretend the couch is a car, and if they let you get them to the car they have to do the dishes. Go over different "what if" scenarios with them to keep them thinking. Insist they go everywhere with a friend and stick to it; don't leave the friend alone even for a second. Let them know it is okay to talk to strangers if you are with them, but to not talk or listen to a stranger if they are alone.

The 1983 television movie about Adam Walsh stuck with me as a child. The kidnapping and murder of Jennifer Wilson in 1988 in Flagstaff, Arizona, actually changed my life. I was born and raised in Flagstaff and my father was the chief of police of the Flagstaff Police Department when Jennifer was abducted. Now that I am a parent to three children, what happened to Adam and Jennifer haunts me even more. The one good thing that can be said of both of their situations is that the disappearance of those beautiful, precious children has saved the lives of countless others as a result of the changes that were made by our parents and schools. Police officers came to my school and talked to us about "stranger danger." Photos of missing children were put on the sides of milk cartons, and my mom would warn me when I went out to play to be careful so my face didn't end up on a milk carton. Looking back now, I didn't understand what that all meant; it was confusing and vague. We need to do better for our children, to stop *talking* to them about staying safe and start *teaching* them how to stay safe.

After attending the execution in 2011 of Jennifer Wilson's convicted killer, I knew if I could do something to save even one child and family from going through what they endured, my life would have purpose.

CHAPTER 9
TEEN TRAUMA
BY TRAVIS WEBB, LMSW

Think of a time when you held a newborn infant. Maybe it was your own newborn. Think of how she felt in your arms. Think of her size, weight, appearance. Think of how soft her hands and cheeks were. Our senses, in that moment, experience great pleasure. We soften our voices, our touch is slow and gentle, and we may even express some emotion. We consciously or subconsciously recognize we are in the presence of perfect innocence. There is no anger, resentment, bitterness, or hopelessness in new infants. They don't hold grudges and manipulate for control. They love and they trust. Our "experience account" is literally at zero at life's commencement, and yet as humans we love and trust inherently. Each of us, without exception, was that perfectly innocent newborn at one point. Through our acquisition of knowledge and experience, we develop traits from our environment. We respond and react to others in a way that others have responded and reacted to us. It is a natural process between infants and caregivers. For example, if a child cries and the caregiver responds lovingly, that child will begin to associate security and love with the caregiver. The opposite can also be true, obviously. This is not an attempt to criticize or blame caretakers' efforts. Rather, it is the mere recognition that little children sponge up their environments.

Why Teens Fail...

We are a product of our life experiences. We start off innocent, but our negative experiences that go unresolved create emotional baggage that inhibits our potential for peace and happiness.

What To Fix...

As parents, we need to create as many positive emotional experiences as possible with our kids to help them develop a healthy self-concept.

WTF

This process continues as the child grows. Children develop foundations based upon the interactions, attention. and affection they receive. This is the part where parents start to worriedly search their efforts for instances when they have done or are doing something to "ruin" their child. Again, this is not parental target practice. Parents, caretakers, teachers, and mentors must recognize that despite their most genuine efforts, each child will face some level of individual, interpersonal, or external trauma. I have sat in my office with distressed parents or teachers who are making every effort to assure a child that they are concerned and committed to helping at all costs. They love those children. They want the best for those children. It is a noble and selfless cause to be a nurturing influence in a child's life. Millions of people can attest to that based upon their own upbringing. That being said, I also recognize those who have been horribly mistreated by adults. I recognize the neglected and the tortured. These are victims of isolated and/or incessant abuse. These young people can become very emotionally injured adults. Many of my clients will instinctively reflect upon their own adverse childhood or adolescent events which they feel led to their current state of adult dysfunction. They stagger through life battling anxiety, anger, depression, or fear. Sadly, their attempts at coping with the pain sometimes involve masking reality with artificial securities (promiscuity, alcohol, prescription or illegal drug abuse, etc.) that are neither lasting nor healing. In fact, for some people it only leads to addiction and shame, recycling their pain over and over again. It's like putting Band-Aids on cancer. However, there are many surviving trauma victims fighting to cope and live healthy lives. They do their best to listen to family and friends telling them to "get over it" or "just let it go" because after all, "it happened a long time ago." This advice can be helpful for few and incredibly discouraging for the rest. They have tried to forgive the past. Many have even tried to build strong relationships with the people who hurt them. They try to let go. But forgiving and being able to let go can be two very different things. When we can intentionally forgive and physiologically let go, we can emotionally heal. We can again love and trust in a way we inherently did as infants.

Why Teens Fail...

Many teens (and adults) are truly attempting to get through past and present events that led to trauma. Statements like "get over it" and "just let it go" don't usually help... at all.

What To Fix...

Each parent must uniquely discern what their child in emotional crisis needs. A silent hug of empathy? Or a firm reminder of the bigger picture? Learn your child's unique emotional storage, coping, and releasing patterns.

WTF

To lay a foundation, I share one client's story of what she experienced at the hands of degenerate individuals while in her teenage years. I hope it brings insight to struggling parents and teens. Obviously, the names and events have been altered to protect the identities of the people involved.

Client: Renee. Female, mid-thirties. Currently married with children.

Reason(s) for seeking therapy: Having trouble feeling at peace, especially concerning some incidents that happened to her several years ago. Anxiety, nervousness.

When asked if she could recount the incidents, she mentioned two specific events. Her body language immediately disclosed that these were horrifying for her to talk about. At age fifteen Renee was raped by her seventeen-year-old boyfriend in a back bedroom at a party. He told her a group of her friends were watching a movie in the bonus room down the hall at his best friend's house—a house that he knew. Intuitively, something inside her told her not to separate from the group, even if her friends were back there. Upon entering an empty bedroom, she was immediately triggered to turn and get out, but unfortunately, it was too late. He "hugged her tight and walked her backward to the bed." He told her he "liked her a lot" and that he was just "really turned on," and "didn't want to hurt her." We've seen Hollywood's depiction of such a scene. Maybe you've even premeditated on what you would do if something like this happened to you. Regardless, she didn't kick him in the groin or gouge his eyes or scream or call the cops. Instead, she froze.

WTF

Why Teens Fail...

Many adults have some unresolved trauma in their lives, be it physical or emotional. Unresolved (stored) trauma can inhibit our ability to nurture our children through potentially traumatic events in their lives.

What To Fix...

Perhaps you can think of a traumatic event in your past in which you "froze."

Recognize and respect this as a potentially system-saving response.

Freezing, for some people, can be as terrifying as the event itself. Have you ever had the nightmare where you see something terrible happening and you can't move or yell for help? When the body messages the mind that it cannot remove or escape a threat, it shuts down to conserve energy, and in a very real sense, it prepares for death. Little children are especially susceptible to this tactic the body uses when they experience physical, sexual, or verbal abuse. Resisting or escaping a much larger adult is rarely an option for a helpless child. Instead they begin to dissociate from the abuser, the pain, and eventually from reality. Renee recalls being totally immobile during the incident. Not just physically immobile, but mentally immobile as well. Her nervous system overrode her "able" sympathetic response. In other words, she did not fight or flee, she froze. Her mind did something similar. She recounts, "My eyes were affixed on the window across the room. I remember my vision getting blurry and realized I was crying, but my brain wouldn't kick-start my body and get me away from him. My muscles felt clinched. I just sat there." When the overwhelming incident ended and she regained mobility, she started to walk home alone. Interestingly, the numbness she felt didn't thaw into panicked shock immediately. She went from not being able to physically or mentally function to not believing what had just happened. In fact, she convinced herself it hadn't really happened and that things were fine between her and her boyfriend, although it was minutes after the rape. She didn't tell anyone about it for months. While these are different responses to the event (*not moving* during the attack, and *not believing* after it ended), they are similar in that they manifest the dissociation of the body from the mind, and the mind from reality, when our nervous system brims to its capacity.

In a subsequent session with Renee, I learned of another incident that was contributing to her present state of anxiety. Three years after the rape, she was at home with a much younger sibling watching television. She went into the kitchen for something when she noticed a man climbing through the trees and over the wall into her backyard. At first glance, she presumed it to be her teenage brother. Quickly, it became obvious that it wasn't her brother, or anyone she knew for that matter. It was an intruder. Again, she felt the life drain out of her and she froze. She didn't scream or run or lock the door or call the police. She stood, knees locked, with tears welling. It was dusk so she could see out the windows, and fortunately, with the lights on inside, he could see *in* the windows. He

Why Teens Fail...

One coping mechanism that many people subconsciously experience is disassociation from the traumatic event. This may lead to denial of the event itself.

What To Fix...

There are several effective ways to help people release trauma (even forgotten trauma) that has been stored in the body. You will be a more effective parent if you take advantage of some form of trauma release therapy.

quickly jumped back over the wall, realizing he had been spotted. I remember her telling me with trembling in her voice, "He could have walked in the back door and ransacked the house. I would have stood there crying."

I think it's important at this junction to stop and process what you might be feeling right now as you read this. Do you feel tense? Do you feel irritated or sad? Recognize your own emotional and physical response as you picture these frightening scenes. Perhaps you feel no sadness for this victim. You might be thinking, "That's nothing compared to what happened to me." Despite what is or isn't flooding through you right now, it is crucial that we never assume trauma impacts two people the same. These experiences, along with all other experiences, are entirely relative to the victims who live through them. What is terrifying and debilitating to one person may not be to the next. It is not our place to judge or interpret someone's mental, emotional, spiritual, or physical reaction to what they've been through or are presently going through. This is true for parents in particular. There is a tendency for parents to tell their children, "I know how you feel" or "I went through that too." While similarities undoubtedly will manifest, children, especially adolescents, must be free to express independently and within their identity when it comes to their personal strife. Can you remember a parent or adult telling you they had been through "the exact same thing" when they were your age? What was *your* response? As parents, with only the best intentions, we want our kids to learn from our mistakes and our heartbreaks. But when we attempt to absorb their pain into our past, we convey a message that their experiences are subordinate to a life already lived and lessons already learned.

WTF

A more effective approach to assisting their recovery involves listening without interrupting, asking empathetic questions about what *they* are feeling, and keeping our stories off center stage. When parents support and encourage the power their children already possess to get through tough times, the child develops healthy coping skills and healthy strategies for solving problems. The parent becomes a trusted ally and a resource for the future. Remember, trauma works respective to the individual

> ## Why Teens Fail...
> Teenagers need to fit in. In an attempt to seem "normal to their peers, they will fight to keep the issue deep down and out of sight. This increases the potential for emotional isolation.

> ## What To Fix...
> Planned communication time provides opportunities for teens to speak openly without fear of being ambushed.

regardless of how anyone interprets the response. It is relative.

Here's a vivid example. Imagine two soldiers fighting side by side in the trenches of war. Together they witness a scene of horrendous carnage that goes on for months. By most people's standards, neither of these soldiers should be the same after living through such unnerving events. And yet, at war's end, one soldier returns to his home town and adjusts well to civilian life. Maybe he starts a family and goes to school. He holds a job and is well liked. He can even share details of his war stories without too much distress. His compatriot, on the other hand, returns home severely disturbed. He has frequent nightmares and waking recollections of the atrocities he lived through. Loud noises, such as commercial planes flying overhead, cause him to crouch instinctively in fear. His exaggerated state of distress results in isolation from a career and lasting relationships. It's clear that Soldier #2 is suffering from post-traumatic stress disorder. Any armchair therapist could easily diagnose it. But the question is why? Why did Soldier #1 adjust so well? Didn't he also see it? Did it not register? Did he do something to cope differently? Why does one have the debilitating symptoms of trauma and the other doesn't seem traumatized at all? Some forms of therapy would examine the differences in the support systems each has in place. Some would investigate history and mental health. All of these could be significant contributing factors to how someone processes the stress resulting from survived traumatic events.

Because symptoms happen primarily in the mind (or so it seems) of an individual suffering from PTSD, several therapeutic methods approach trauma strictly psychologically. We have learned that this is only half of the story at best. I've heard it a hundred times: "I *know* what I need to do and I do it, but I don't *feel* better." Notice the words know and feel. I recognize that we use these terms loosely, but I sense there is significance in how people attempt to describe the state of the mind (what they know) and the body (what they feel). Many trauma

---

Why Teens Fail...

What is traumatic to one person may not be traumatic to another person and vice versa. Different people have different life experiences, different social support systems, and different coping mechanisms.

What To Fix...

Maybe your trauma doesn't seem as monumental as another person's trauma. This simply indicates that you are a different individual with different storage and releasing mechanisms.

survivors have learned the strategies, but the symptoms remain. What the *body* does during and after the traumatic event is monumental in understanding why people get stuck in their symptoms.

Dr. Peter Levine, an expert on trauma, states:

> Trauma is fundamentally a highly activated incomplete biological response to threat, frozen in time. For example, when our full neuromuscular and metabolic machinery prepares us to fight or to flee, muscles throughout the entire body are tensed in specific patterns of high-energy readiness. When we are unable to complete the appropriate actions and discharge the tremendous energy generated by our survival preparations, this energy becomes fixated into specific patterns of neuromuscular readiness. Afferent feedback to the brain stem generated from these incomplete neuromuscular/autonomic responses maintains a state of acute and then chronic arousal and dysfunction in the central nervous system. Traumatized people are not suffering from a disease in the normal sense of the word. They have become fixated in an aroused state. It is difficult (if not impossible) to function normally under these circumstances.

Why Teens Fail...

The basic human instinct is to take flight or fight when faced with potential trauma. When neither of these options manifest, we are prone to freeze.

What To Fix...

Identify moments or periods of life when you (or someone you love) was physically or emotionally "frozen" in the face of a trauma. There are methods for releasing the stored energy that leads to trauma.

Let's step back and really break this down. When we experience a threat, our mind tells our body to ready itself for fighting or fleeing in an energetic state. The muscles tense, heart rate increases, breathing quickens, and senses become sharp. If we are unable to move proactively (and this can be physically, mentally, or emotionally) and discharge the built-up energy, it becomes stored.

The brain receives the message that the "ready switch" is on and it's not shutting off. Instead of moving from rest (parasympathetic) to ready (sympathetic) and back to rest, we get stuck in that heightened state. And if fighting with rage or sprinting for safety doesn't bring about the change necessary for the central nervous system to return things to a rested state, what follows is the system's third and final option: dissociation, disconnection, shutting down, or numbness (frozen). And again, this can be physical, mental, or emotional.

At this point our resting baseline is shifted way up somewhere between disconnected and utter terror. Looking again at Renee's response to being raped, we can identify these responses. First, she *intuitively* sensed that isolation from the rest of the group would lead to something dangerous. Had she followed that intuition, she might have avoided the attack. Never discredit, never ignore your gut instinct. You may not know you were right for following it (because the incident is averted), but you will always know when you were wrong for ignoring it. Second, upon entering the bedroom, she didn't ask where everyone was or what he was up to. She *tried to flee*. He blocked her attempt at leaving the room by grabbing her and then walking her to the bed. Third, *unable* to remove or run from the threat, her system blew right through the fight-or-flight response and went directly to freeze. For whatever reason, it was triggered almost immediately in her. Remember, not all people are the same in this regard. Renee spent years in counseling. She saw three different (very capable) therapists. She was referred to me by one of those therapists who had given her numerous strategies, skills, and information for healing. Her therapist wisely recognized that Renee's physiological self was stuck, and that she needed psycho-physiological therapy. The brain struggled to implement the strategies she had learned until the body could discharge what it was holding from years past. This is why it can be so difficult to let go.

Why Teens Fail...

Our senses operate on a conscious and a subconscious level. When we ignore these subconscious perceptions, sometimes called "intuition," we may be placing ourselves in harm's way.

What To Fix...

As previous chapters of this book have illustrated, we need to listen to our inner voice, our intuition, or that part of us that perceives danger at a subconscious level.

When I met Renee, the rape had happened more than twenty years prior. Imagine living in an anxious state for more than twenty years. Some don't need to imagine. You might be thinking of your own experiences at this point. Maybe some of this is ringing true for your struggling teen. We must recognize and be empathetic to where our loved ones are when it comes to trauma. Never assume that your child is overreacting or just being dramatic when they tell you they feel numb. Frequent manifestations of anxiety or anger in a teenager may be the resulting state of a traumatic event. Renee's story is an extreme example of a rape victim who had a clear "freeze" response. We need not assume that she froze strictly based on the horrific nature of rape. It does not require such an incident to traumatize a person. Many people seeking therapy in my office have not been to war or victims of abusive crimes. They are individuals who have had "uncommon" responses to "common" events. We've all experienced some level of loss (death, divorce, relocation, etc.), rejection (peer groups, dating, work-related, etc.), or suffering. Many of us move in, through, and out of these events without serious troubles or residual effects. Many of us don't. At sixteen years old, a breakup, for example, can send a teen into a tailspin, diminishing self-esteem and skyrocketing anxiety—even though the forty-six year-old parent may know their teenager will "get over it." I have come to realize that "getting over it" for most people means *mentally numbing* until the memory is less present and *physically storing* and living with the pain. Teens need their parents to listen without giving the answer. Remember, your molehills might be their mountains.

> ## Why Teens Fail...
>
> *Some adolescents lack experience with wading through loss, rejection, or suffering (all of which are part of living). You know it's not the end of the world, but they aren't so sure.*

So what's the answer to discharging all this trapped energy? A long run? A punching bag? For many people, physical movement such as workouts and manual labor can help alleviate much of the problem. Think of how you feel after a good workout. Typical results include internal energy, happiness, and a restoration. We feel these because of the discharging process of this trapped, negative energy. The body feels lighter and more energetic when we aren't *spending our energy to hold our energy.* I use a specific bodywork modality to help people rid the body of this storage. It involves a few stretches and exercises that isolate and moderately fatigue certain muscle groups. When the body is placed in a rested position following these exercises, it begins to lightly tremor or shake. This type of tremor is neurogenic. It is different than what you

> ## What To Fix...
>
> *Good therapists help their clients self-discover answers to their problems. Good parents do the same.*
>
> *Don't be afraid to seek help if any of these points sound familiar. You're not alone.*

feel following excessive physical activity. Too much exertion can expend more energy than there is oxygen and result in lactic acid buildup in the muscles. Neurogenic tremors, on the other hand, are what you feel after an overwhelming event. Everyone has felt neurogenic tremors before. Think of what your body does as you stand to speak in public, or during a scary movie. On a much grander scale, think of what your body does after a car accident, or a life-threatening event. Mothers, what about after giving birth? In each of these instances *our bodies shake or tremble.* This is how the human body is designed to discharge large amounts of energy. Animals do the exact same thing. Cognitively, our brains have greater capacities than animals, but neurologically we are very similar. If would-be prey in the wild escapes a predator, it will neurogenically tremor, then go back to a habitual existence. Because of this, animals don't have many of the same problems humans do. You don't see zebras lying under a tree months after a survived attack feeling significant amounts of anxiety, anger, or depression. They immediately and instinctually expend the build-up. Energy floods the body in preparation for survival, but if the body doesn't spend this energy *during* the event, it must discharge the energy *after* the event. And if it can't discharge after, obviously, the energy stays in the body. Crying and laughing are more common ways we discharge this surmounting of energy. Notice what your body does when you really cry hard or laugh hysterically. We kind of bounce, or quiver, or convulse, depending on the situation and severity. We emit sound and tears. Now think of how you feel physically after a good cry or laugh. We feel better because we discharge a ton of energy. When our system is brimming, we feel it. We are tense, sensitive, and emotional. As distress signals are processed in that state, we cry easily (or laugh, or laugh until we cry, or cry until we laugh) to spill some of the surplus. The brain knows the difference between laughing and crying, but the body doesn't. It is an organism that responds to the demands of the mind and the environment it exists in.

Why Teens Fail...

Embarrassment or shame can result from "chronic crying." Shame is counterproductive and often exacerbates the underlying problem.

What To Fix...

The body is like a reservoir. When that reservoir fills to the brim with the stress we are trying to process, it will spill. Crying is a common way we discharge energy.

I like to use the analogy that our body is one of those monthly rental storage units, and the brain is the manager that sits at the gate. When you pull up with your truckload of stress or trauma, you must first consult with the manager. He assesses the size of the load, then recommends a unit large enough to accommodate all of your items easily. Some people are okay with this and proceed to the designated space to unload. They stack it in carefully in an organized manner, close the door, lock up, and leave. Others feel that they don't *really* need the larger, more expensive option so they go with a smaller unit. They pack it in floor to ceiling, wall to wall. They lean on the bulk and force the rolling door down, lock it up, and leave. Sometimes the storage unit remains loaded for decades, literally.

WTF

Why Teens Fail...

Over our lifetimes, we can amass and store a significant amount of traumatic events in the "storage unit" of our physical bodies. This causes stress and can lead to emotional distress or disease.

Likewise, we need to discharge energy in the body. We also need to let it flow out of the mind. I want to share one more story from a client. Hopefully it adds to my point.

What To Fix...

Releasing stored, negative energy from our "storage unit" can seem overwhelming or even terrifying to some people. Take it one box at a time.

Client: James, forty to forty-five years old, married (third marriage)

Reasons for seeking therapy: "Sometimes feel a little frustrated, but I'm okay."

James was referred to me by a friend who is a yoga instructor. She told me he was a really nice guy who got along with everyone, but seemed disturbed inside. The first time I spoke with James about meeting for a session, it was over the phone. I remember his voice was energetic and resolute, but barely audible. He wanted to keep the conversation concise and very private. We quickly set up an appointment. When James walked in that next week, I immediately noticed how fit he was for his age. I also noticed, however, how coiled he carried himself. His shoulders were scrunched up just below his ears, like he had a severe kink in the entirety of his neck. I asked him about any recent accidents, injuries, or tension. He almost looked startled at the question. "No, I don't think so," he replied. When I mentioned his shoulders, he informed me that he hadn't really noticed how high he carries them. I made a mental note to investigate any dissociation from the body he might manifest later. We got to know each other for a few minutes by talking briefly about his marriages and kids. He told me his previous attempts at marriage had failed in similar fashion. He said, "They loved me but complained that they didn't know me, and it caused trust issues." Suddenly and without my asking, he started to tell me his history by saying, "I've literally never told a soul any of this. But I have to tell someone before it kills me."

I encouraged him to let it out. He and his younger brother had had a very rough childhood (to put it lightly). His dad was gone and his mom was a heavy drug user and a prostitute who worked out of their apartment. Every type of debased activity imaginable happened to James and his little brother in those early years. He hesitated at some of the more difficult details during his story, but it was clear he needed to say it all, so I prompted him forward. His mother used him as she needed him. Can you imagine a mother sending her seven-year-old down to the gas station with cash to pick up her next hit? Or to escort men in off the street? The men who came through mistreated the two boys in cruel ways. Their mother was not there to comfort, console, or defend them in any way. Often, as the older brother, James tried in vain to protect his younger brother from having to be part of it. With his strong personality, he never allowed anyone to know what was happening at home. He lied to teachers, neighbors, and friends. He kept it all to himself. Having done home visits as a current school administrator, I am sure many people knew a large portion of what was happening in James's life, but James would not be the one to disclose it. Mercifully, he and his brother were taken from his mother by Child Protective Services for reasons of neglect when he was eleven. They were placed with a foster family. He conjured a story up for them too. I don't know if the foster family ever knew the truth or not.

Why Teens Fail...

Big or small, your stored trauma will continue to reside in you if not discharged. It can manifest itself, wreaking havoc on the physical and emotional beings.

What To Fix...

This chapter relies on some extreme examples of trauma that had lasting effects on these clients. Your trauma may seem more or less significant to you than those depicted here. Trauma is relative.

I can remember truly feeling his pain as he talked. Up to that point in my short career, I had heard several stories of abuse and neglect, but this one seemed to top them all. His story was terribly sad, and I remember feeling that common desire to travel back in time to rescue those two little boys from their mother. But the thing that was most difficult for me that day was to learn he had never spoken to anyone about his story prior to that moment. And this is my point in sharing this story. James was married to a wonderful woman and had been married twice before. None of his wives knew any of it. His kids didn't know anything about their father's upbringing. His closest friends didn't know. He wouldn't even talk to his brother about it. This poor man had been carrying this difficult load, completely alone, for more than thirty years. He lived with pain and sorrow packed to the very core of his being. He didn't want to burden anyone with what he felt as he made every effort to "be normal" around others. He didn't want anyone to treat him differently, and hoped the pain and sorrow would eventually fade from memory. Quite honestly, if I were in his shoes, I would have hoped to forget what happened too. Again, maybe the way James responded to his trauma is hitting close to home for some people reading this. Suddenly, the quiet voice on the phone, the scrunched shoulders, and the failed marriages started to make more sense. He tried to protect everyone around him from having to feel an ounce of what he lived with. Hours were spent in the gym running, lifting, pushing, and pulling in an attempt to burn up some of the stored energy. Honestly, it's probably how he survived as long as he did. His body was muscular, but obviously tense and brimming with harrowing memories of his childhood. We did bodywork after a couple sessions of psychotherapy. The floodgates opened as the tremors raced through his body. We met several times, and each session was filled with more hope, and a little less pain. It was nothing short of miraculous to watch this man finally start to heal. He had to let it out. He had to tell his story. He had to let the body tell its story.

Why Teens Fail...

As parents, we sometimes have trauma that inhibits our ability to be effective parents.

What To Fix...

All of these principles apply equally to adults or teens who may be in crisis as a result of trauma.

More than likely any parent reading this has more investment in their child than someone like James's mother did. But we can learn so much from the people who faced such circumstances. Adolescents can develop lines of love and trust when they can talk from the heart about childhood to someone who loves them enough to trust *their* interpretation of *their* experience. Of course we want our children to listen to what we are saying. They would struggle without the guidance. But we must be willing to listen to them. We must trust them as they try to trust themselves. We must let them tell us where and why it hurts.

Health is not a buried treasure at the end of a lost trail. While learning life skills and coping strategies offer immense benefits to all seeking them, we must remember the capacity each adolescent life *already* holds. We must remember our inherent state of loving and trusting. It is in each and every one of us. We must allow ourselves to feel and heal. We must allow others the space to do the same. We can love and trust as adolescents and adults when we can move in, through, and out of trauma. This requires taking off the heavy cloaks of learned dysfunction that we put on over the years, and allowing the person at the core to re-emerge.

CHAPTER 10

QUALITY COMMUNICATION:
FAMILY DYNAMICS

BY SHANNON BUTLER, COMMUNICATION INSTRUCTOR AND MIDDLE SCHOOL TEACHER

Who are we? In each role we play a different part, as if on stage, and adjust our communication style accordingly. I am a daughter, a sister, a friend, a wife, a mother, a role model, a parent, a home owner, an educator, a Phoenician, an Arizonan, a United States citizen, and a caring inhabitant of this world. Each role carries different responsibilities, adopting different perspectives and connecting us to a variety of *in-groups* (groups from which we identify). The communication patterns within each role directly impact our interpersonal relationships with others; communication is the glue that helps bind our relationships, much like the chapters of this book. I truly believe strong communication is the most important skill we can pass on to our children and model within our families, while remembering we too are learning to manage our lives within the different roles we play! In this chapter, I am grateful to share with you my educational, teaching, and parenting experiences, along with a spoonful of spiced sugar just to help the medicine go down.

WTF

"It is through our interactions, be they successful or disastrous, whether they generate hardship or create harmony, that make us better people; these interactions allow us to grow, learn, and cherish those with which we interact." I dedicate this chapter to

> ## Why Teens Fail...
>
> *Many if not all relationship failures are a direct result of a failure in communication. We either fail to communicate our needs or fail to understand the needs of our relationship partners.*

> ## What To Fix...
>
> *Take time to learn or relearn a few key communication skills. They are simple in theory yet require practice in order to put them to good use.*

all of my students, teen and adult alike; my two sons, Antony and Ashton; and my supportive husband, Martin, the true writer in the family—you are a valuable reflection of my self-concept. LOL: I truly love you all; thank you for illuminating my world!

—*Shannon D. B. Butler*

BTFB: Back to Family Basics: You Are Rock Stars! You Are Already Doing So Much RIGHT!

True Story: Knights of the Round Table

Why Teens Fail...

Parents are very good at talking AT their kids rather than WITH their kids. Good communication is at least half LISTENING.

What To Fix...

Family dinner is an excellent place to practice listening to your kids. Family dinner is a lost ritual. Those who practice it know it is a great place to ask your kids to tell you something interesting about their day...every day!

I have taught different subjects such as communication, social studies, and english for a total of sixteen years; I've become theatrical and very communication-oriented within my own household and classrooms. Raising two boys and instructing thousands of teen and adult learners, I've learned to wear various hats such that of a knight, an advisor, a role model, a spy, a queen, a prime minister, and yes, even a superhero. Chivalry and heroism are not dead, especially in my household. I've officially found my place and have become Wonder Woman, literally! Really, I am not joking; I have the cape and Wonder Woman outfit, now I just need the bulletproof armbands to go with it, but instead of deflecting bullets, I deflect poor communication rituals. I am aware of the art of listening, where each member of a communication interaction should have equal time speaking and listening. I also know that nonverbal communication is more accurate than the spoken word about 65 percent of the time. Teaching communication to college students over the past ten years has allowed me to extend this knowledge and understanding to my eighth graders and family, since I appreciate that listening is a learned skill. The climate within a communication interaction is imperative; any quality communication skill includes good listening!

Bearing all this in mind, and recalling that I am Wonder Woman, it only made sense for me to swoop into my home and save my family dinners. I instated King Arthur's Nights of the Round Table into our lives. Our former table was a long rectangular shape and didn't meet our family's needs when sharing our day together—the art of proxemics. "What was your favorite thing that happened to you today dear?" I would ask each family member as if shouting down a long tunnel (while wind blew back my cape, of course). Since the new "round" table arrived, I have noticed the effect I had hoped for: better communication. I have a closer view of my children's nonverbal behaviors, as they fidget to stay away from certain topics, use their body language to explore their words, or exaggerate their stories with humor. The table helped establish a better climate for listening. My boys enjoy sharing with us their favorite and worst moment of their day. Storytelling has become more of a ritual, and it has become much easier to listen to each other with the shape of the table and with a closer proximity. Now I wonder how much I missed for years in truly listening to my family. A kitchen table is not just about the food! Now, each night, I sit at the table with my family, look at my husband, and smile. He'll ask, "What?" and I'll respond, "I LOVE this kitchen table."

Professional Analysis

Our society has taught our children to challenge information: debate, rebut, compete, tweet, and question. It is the American way. Communicative competition is embedded through our capitalistic society, and it doesn't always allow for good communication skills to flourish. Sometimes our teens don't distinguish between questioning issues and behaviors versus questioning adults or people's character traits. It's confusing to them when they watch politicians verbally accost one another, or hear about the latest Hollywood star behaving in poor ways and explaining their actions with equally poor communication skills. After all, these people have a large platform for modeling these behaviors to our youth.

> **Why Teens Fail...**
>
> *Teens rarely say, "I made a poor choice today, and I'm fearful to share it with you. I'd like you to listen to me in a way that you would have liked to have been listened to when you were my age. Please tell me when would be a good time to talk."*

> **What To Fix...**
>
> *We need to teach our teens how to communicate with scripts like the one above, for example. Then we need to be ready to listen without a knee-jerk emotional reaction so that they keep coming back in the future.*

Yikes: Sex, drugs, and slander, baby! As members of a community, whether we are grandparents, parents, or educators, it is up to us to model these good communication skills. Our teens are taught to hear and not listen, to turn their ears off in order to compete for their words to be heard first. We live in an individualistic society where the individual needs come first instead of the collective group, the whole group (family needs). We are taught to promote ourselves in order to be on top, and yet we tell our teens to be humble and not to be so self-centered or self-absorbed. Many of the messages society sends our children can come across as mixed messages when you consider the above examples. No wonder our society is confused; there are contradictions everywhere! Having a forum, a safe place, for modeling appropriate communication skills, like at the kitchen table, can only help families develop strong communication patterns where teens can understand our world. Embedded family rituals where every family member shares parts of their day, connects with triumphs and troubles, explores current events, is held accountable, and shares discussions littered with common values provide parents with opportunities to reinforce positive self-concepts in our children. These are just some of the reasons that every family would love to eat at the Round Table, too. After all, we are the superhero of our own lives. Only we can take on that leading role and model it!

Why Teens Fail...

Teens are faced with a barrage of double standards in our society as it is. Mom can smoke, but you can't. Dad can drink, but you can't. I can yell at you, but you can't yell at me.

What To Fix...

Family communication rituals such as dinnertime discussions give us a place and a forum to practice expressing good family values without criticism and to model good communication skills.

WTF

Strategies to Succeed

Exhale! Exhale! Exhale! These are the fundamentals in being a parent, much like the three rules of real-estate (only sorry, you can't resell your child!). Truly, we have to pat ourselves on the back because no one loves or advocates for our teens more than we do. Celebrate the list of good communication strategies you are already imbedding into your family, much like my family's Round Table.

Pre-Established Family Ground Rules:

Evidence of Concrete Communication: Contracts/written agreements for important responsibilities with embedded rewards (other than money). Allowing privileges ONLY as positive reinforcements for expected behaviors. Examples: movies with friends, sleepovers, Xbox and PlayStation usage, cell phone usage, including texting, iPod allowances for downloading music, paintball, laser tag, Facebook usage, skate park, hanging with friends, etc. As parents, we realize and remember these extras are just that—privileges—and at any time they can be taken away.

Nonreactive Listening: Our teens are learning and growing rapidly (just take a look at your grocery bill). All of this physical and psychological growth takes a great toll on them. Combine this information with today's involved teen, who is busier than ever, and you will find most skills in hearing only. Listening, for them and for you, isn't easy. Thank you for being a good listener to your teen, asking clarifying questions that are open-ended and allow your children to elaborate, evaluate, and process their own thoughts out loud to you without judgment. You are the type of parent who does not disguise questions to teach your teen a lesson (also known as counterfeit questioning, a barrier to listening). Instead, you use silent listening, a process of attending to words and information then sorting them into recognizable patterns of meaning, thus developing pictures in your mind. You stay responsive nonverbally and focus on words. You know that meanings are in not in words, they are in people. As a parent, you limit emotional reactionary responses, take deep breaths, or perhaps drink a glass of wine and maintain your composure. You know how to empathize with your teen's needs and issues. Being a mindful listener can only empower your child and model a competent skill set for them to follow. In essence, you do not allow your emotions to drive your communication responses.

> ## Why Teens Fail...
> *Our children learn from our examples, for better or for worse. When we model inappropriate or ineffective communication skills, our children will almost certainly mimic those examples at some later date.*

> ## What To Fix...
> *Utilize "nonreactive listening" or "silent listening," a process of attending to words, sounds, and information while limiting emotionally reactionary responses.*

Taking Care of Yourself as Individuals: As parents, we have our own responsibilities and merely listing them—caring for our family, our household, career/profession, appointments, health care, educating our children, etc. —falls very short of explaining those responsibilities. Now add to your list of responsibilities two, three, or four children, perhaps other dependents such as a grandparent who now need help from you with their household, health issues, etc. Sometimes we have more to deal with than is humanly possible, and it can cause cracks in the foundation of our communication skills with those who are most important, our family members. To deal with these numerous tasks, we use the following simple techniques: counting backward from 10 to 1 until we are calm, taking a twenty-minute nap or a bath, exercising, maybe having another glass of wine, exercising, enjoying a hot cup of tea with a conversation, doing yoga, taking a date night, exercising, perhaps having a girl's night out or guy cave time. People with strong self-confidence and self-concept have parents who model patience and find childproof dumpsters in which to release their stress, a place to scrape off their piled-high plate. You know that your teens are not paper towels that absorb all of your troubles. Appreciating and rejuvenating ourselves as individuals and partners helps to maintain better communication skills with less psychological noise (e.g., conflict with someone else, or too low or high of a self-concept) or physiological noise (e.g., hunger, sickness, tiredness) that can easily disrupt the communication process and interpretation of messages.

Why Teens Fail...

When parents fail to take time to communicate with each other (about relationship items as well as task items), their relationship will almost certainly suffer. This suffering is inevitably passed on to the children or teens.

What To Fix...

Parents need to take time for themselves. They need to have weekly or biweekly date nights at a minimum. Keeping the romance alive will make life more fun and fulfilling for the kids too!

Scripts through Storytelling: You are proactive and think in measures of *when* to communicate at a quality level. Maybe it's driving your teen to school or picking them up, shooting hoops, or painting nails; perhaps it's that kitchen table! You share the lessons you've learned through narratives. These stories are your family rituals that will be remembered when your child encounters a similar situation in the future. These stories can help guide their reactions, responses, decisions, and communication within their interpersonal (one-on-one) relationships. These stories also contribute to the family's identity, humor, and fun; they reflect on the roles each member plays and affirm personal values established by the family as a small group. Every family has their own personal stories that are enjoyable to hear over and over again!

WTF

Your Perception Is NOT Your Child's Reality!
True Story: Facebook over Face-to-Face?

I remember when my father bought my family our first computer in the early '80s. He said, "This will save us time!" And it did, for a decade or so. By the '90s we questioned whether it really did save time, as we were slowly sucked into the Internet or what I like to call "the helium effect." What fun we had as we learned to surf the net with new voices and different levels of disclosure! Computer-mediated communication evolved into so much more as we became Googlers, eBayers, Amazonians, gamers, Facebookers, Tweeters, etc. The interest level and easy access to information and communication gave us a high! Thus the information age came to life and the twenty-first century consumed us all, especially teens. Since the information age, access to any kind of information comes in numerous venues and can be extremely time consuming. We are addicted. I spoke to one of my eighth grade students, Gabi, about it, and she shared a comparison between her and her mother's teenage experience.

"When my mother was growing up, she and her friends did not Skype, text, or Facebook like people do today. My mom and her friends actually got together. They rode their bikes around the neighborhood and were always active outside. Today, friends rarely get together outside. People my age only talk and interact online through technology. People Skype rather than meet face to face. They chat and gossip on Facebook. Young people today use technology as their main social network. From my mom's stories and experiences, I have realized how different our generation is than previous generations. The way we communicate and interact with each other is very unlike that of my mom's."

> **Why Teens Fail...**
>
> *Technology designed to create efficiency and improved time management has led to a barrage of all-consuming hobbies that actually make us less productive in many areas than we were before the advent of such technology.*

> **What To Fix...**
>
> *Teach your teens to use technology to increase their efficiency and avoid the pitfalls of allowing technology to waste valuable time that could be spent on another*

Professional Analysis

Considering teens are developing their self-concept based on their set perceptions of the world they live in, including their exposure to and experiences with cyberspace, Facebook, smartphones, bullying, drugs, parties, peer pressure, clubs, expectations at home, expectations from their in-group, school, sports, and other extracurricular activities, their peer group becomes extremely instrumental in their self-concept. Teens will compare themselves to their relevant peer groups, using social comparisons as the very basis for them to evaluate their self-worth. Their self-esteem is delicately balanced between their worlds at home and with peers, where social media and the information age are having a long-standing effect. Add up the hours your teens are with other peer groups in comparison to being home with parents—and I'm not talking about when they are home on a computer-mediated communication (CMC) device or sleeping. When generating percentages, you will understand the tremendous amount of time we are not with our children and how much influence their outside world touches their self-concept. Communication with others in the world today can have a life-long impact on our children as we post to cyberspace and are copied to a thousand friends on Facebook—and yes, these friends then forward the same communication to each of their thousand friends, allowing your teen's communication to now be shared with a million unknown individuals. Our teen's thoughts and emotions are now posted into the cosmos, in a sort of cyber junkyard of permanency where friends, strangers, colleges, and even future employers can sift through this junk and find nuggets of not-so-flattering information. It's a scary decade! We find ourselves in unknown territory as if exploring the universe for the first time, combined with these new ways in which to communicate. One of the biggest problems is learning how to navigate this information age, realizing that our world, though perhaps enhanced or enriched by social media, is still earth, whereas our teen's world is space, together with its limitless uses and misuses, unclear boundaries, and fudged perceptions. How do we prepare them, guide them, protect them as they float in zero gravity with the ever-varying devices technology presents for communicating?

Why Teens Fail...

Our teens' communication skills are filtered through their perception of reality—a reality skewed by a world of cyberspace in which their peers readily engage in innumerable venues of risky behavior such as sexting, bullying, etc.

What To Fix...

Explain to your teens that future employers will conduct extensive background checks on prospective employees, digging up all of the dirt (videos, pics, chat logs, etc.) from a decade of short-sighted Internet sex, drugs, and rock 'n roll.

Strategies to Succeed

In some cases our teens know that adults can't possibly "get it," so please don't establish the mentality of "I get it" within your household. It's okay to admit that we don't know everything; we too are on a learning curve with each new stage our family enters! Your teens will respect you for your honesty, and you will open the doors to communication instead of shutting them down by pretending. We can't possibly live with them in cyberspace, nor would many parents want to. Come back down to earth, inform yourself about these varied CMC devices, and model competent skills. Learn to be a communication partner with them as you and your teen navigate CMC throughout the cosmos.

Is a Text Today Time Thrown Away? It depends on your perception! The twenty-first-century cyber friend, boyfriend, and girlfriend can now enter your household at any moment without your knowledge. They no longer use the home phone or walk through the front door and announce their presence; they just text, call on a cell phone, or use Facebook. They text each other "good morning" while still lying in their beds, they text each other their breakfast choice, they text each other while showering, they text each event of the day. A study by Lisa Tidwell and Joseph Walther (Beebe and Masterson, 2012), found that people in computer-mediated "conversations" asked more direct questions, which resulted in people revealing more, not less, information about themselves when online. The more our teens disclose and are disclosed to, the more we consider it too invasive, an interruption of family time, and a consumption of your teen's leisure or study time. Notice how swiftly your teen finds friends at large functions. Notice how quickly the phone leaps into their hand whenever they leave the house, their room, or the couch. Notice that the devices are ever present, a very necessary comfort and reinforcement for your teen, habitually grabbed, held, and cradled as an infant would their favorite soft toy or blanket.

WTF

Why Teens Fail...

Research shows that when two people speak to one another (communicate face to face), they are only accurately picking up approximately 25–50 percent of each other's behavior. (Adler, et al., 2012).

What To Fix...

*1. Use adjectives to describe the BEHAVIORS you have noticed.
2. Share two possible interpretations of the behavior you have witnessed.
3. Request verbal clarification of their specific behavior and its meaning.
4. Don't make assumptions!*

They communicate so much more because they can: it's easy, it's fast, and it's global! Everything and anything can be interrupted with a small, innocent "blip ding" sound effect and off your teen jumps out of the shower and to the cell phone, disclosing the most personal of information. Your teen is left with unnecessary communication and sharing too much personal information, and parents are left with a wet bathroom floor since there was no time to towel off.

As an educator, I watch twenty-first-century teens and young adults look up resources online, and I have to reintroduce them to a thing called a book. They would prefer to spend hours finding one or two sources online, as they are simultaneously inundated with a torrent of unrelated websites, banners, popups, and ads attempting to sell them products that are loosely connected to their search. As well, at their fingertips is a pool of entertainment, music, games, and videos. Attracted and delayed by the many tributaries, they meander off topic and accomplish little. Often it would take them a fraction of that time, fifteen or twenty minutes, to look up the information in hard copy. I cringe to watch them suffer because they just wasted their time. I'm a strong believer in working smarter, not harder! But they continue and persevere in their addiction to using only online resources, many of which lack validity.

What is acceptable in your household isn't necessarily the norm. I have a neighbor who outlaws any CMC device on Saturdays, and yet another friend who doesn't allow the cell phone to leave the main living area of the home. What will your household rules be to prevent future problems? It's up to the parents to set the expectations and norms early, or conflict will arise.

WTF

Is Technology Today's BLING? NND: Not necessary, Nice to have, but Dangerous for maturing brains. Maybe it's time for a family meeting where you become Super Techie. I can picture your costume already—gray cape, heroic symbol on your chest, and nerd glasses! Some parents know that their child really doesn't need all these extra virtual channels for communicating; a

---

Why Teens Fail...

Parents all too often expect their teens to somehow just know what the family's values are. These parents are often surprised to find out that their teens misperceived any number of attitudes and behaviors to mean something entirely different than intended.

What To Fix...

Take a few minutes to verbalize your ten most important family values with your spouse. Convey these values often to your children through word and deed. Leave little room for ambiguous interpretation on the part of your teen.

certain level of maturity is needed in order to handle and understand the effects of them. After all, the average brain doesn't fully mature until approximately the age of twenty-six. Reality strikes when we realize these varying channels are not going away; rather they are becoming embedded as a social network medium for many teens and adult users in many households and organizations. Some families want their children prepared for the twenty-first century when it comes to computer-mediated communication. In understanding the different venues and how to communicate within these new modalities, each family needs to set rules and create pre-established understandings about the type of communication that is acceptable with each varied path. Family meetings are strong communication rituals that provide the place and planning for these discussions. See Appendix C for a chart to begin your family planning and discussions for clarity in expectations with CMC.

Every communication interaction is delivered from people with different backgrounds and experiences deriving from set perceptions of their world, which shapes their communication with others. Everyone has thousands of individual experiences every single day. We take these experiences with us, like luggage when we go on vacation, except we can't set them down anywhere, we always have them in our hands. All these experiences—the contents of our bags—teach us and help identify who we are, how we want to behave, how we communicate with others, and how to set ourselves up for success or failure. They shape our self-esteem, our thinking, and our problem-solving skills, which culminate into creation of our perceptions. Remember, our reality is handmade by us through our communication skills and our experiences.

Why Teens Fail...

Some teens resort to cutting, self-mutilation, or suicide when they feel that there are no trusted adults to communicate with about their fears, anxieties, or disappointments in life. Sadly enough, I run into several teens each new school year who fall into this category.

Family: Are You *Listening* or Just Hearing?
True Story: Is it Laziness or Something Else?

I have been fortunate to know thousands of students throughout my years of teaching. One such student, Sara, would come to me as her last effort to communicate with an adult; she no longer trusted most adults.

What To Fix...

Parents must be cautious about assuming they know everything that is going on in their teen's life. To avoid making assumptions, conversations should be open, honest, and direct. They should involve much LISTENING on the part of the parents.

WTF

Through the school year, I learned from Sara that she had attempted suicide and was a cutter. Within our conversations, she would always tell me that her parents didn't listen to her. Alarmed by Sara's need to hurt herself and concern for her well-being, I found that this resonated with me. The common statements made by Sara regarding these issues lingered throughout my days and into my evenings. Why would such a beautiful, bright, and outgoing young lady feel the need to attempt such extremes? One day I specifically asked her, "How don't they listen?" Sara shared her thoughts.

"Being a teenager is never easy—always having to deal with schoolwork, drama, siblings, and all of the chores we get at home. However, sometimes you just need to take a break from everything, but if you have misunderstanding parents, this can be taken the wrong way. No, you're not giving up, you're not giving up at all, but if so much is going on in your life that you're distracted, parents can take that as laziness, which it clearly isn't. A few months ago, I was going through a rough time with my life; I had drama with friends, I didn't understand my schoolwork, my boyfriend broke up with me, and I was being bullied everywhere I went. One night during the middle of winter break, my parents called me into their room to have a 'discussion.' Yet this wasn't a discussion at all, but rather a fight because, according to me, screaming at each other isn't a discussion. My parents accused me of things like laziness, stubbornness, and being just plain confused. However, if I tried to explain something, they would simply ignore it. If they didn't like my answers to their questions, I received no listening on their part. To them, I was spoiled rotten and I was taking advantage of them. But to me, I was trying to juggle things in my life that were making school hard to handle and concentrate on. Trying to pay attention in school or at home seemed near impossible. In the end, my parents grounded me and wouldn't let me say anything.

Why Teens Fail...

It is a huge temptation for parents to turn a family discussion into an ambush for the teen. Irrational teen behavior can be perplexing and frustrating to parents who do not see all of the social, academic, and extracurricular pressures their teen faces.

What To Fix...

Just as parents want to be understood by the teen, they should strive to understand the teen by asking open-ended questions about behaviors that appear to be inconsistent with a family's given set of values. Family values can be reinforced at these times.

WTF

"Not to mention, every time I tried to tell them to stop yelling at me (which they told me to do if I found it scary or stressful), they'd raise their voice even louder and say they were not yelling. I have often had moments where I wished I could have something on me to record them so they could listen to how they sound. But I've just gotten to the point where I sit, listen, and apologize just to end the conversation. If it's done and out of the way, it's better than extending it or letting it linger for the rest of the week, just because I foolishly tried sticking up for myself."

Communication is the foundation of all interaction between people. We need it to survive and desire good skills in order to thrive. Sara may be one extreme example, but she is one of many students from middle school to my young adult students who grew up in a household were listening did not occur and the communication rituals embedded into the family foundation were poor.

Professional Analysis

If you think about it, when's the last time your teen has had a tranquil place to just "be"? These days, teens are blasted with information everywhere they go. It seems as if children have more assignments to complete for homework and projects, and more commitments for attendance at parties, sports practice and events, birthdays, recitals, rehearsals, and performances. They simply have more involvement at an earlier age with school and extracurricular activities. Teens have more venues for entertainment, more ways in which their friends can contact them. I'm not sure if many teens would be able to find a healing, solitary serenity, or even know that it can be very good for the mind. For heaven's sake, when you step out of your car prepared to spend money at the mall, they now even have music playing in the parking lot. You can't escape the noise.

What happened to listening to the birds? Remember when your children were babies and sometimes the only thing that would calm their crying was to walk around with them outside? Our teens are slammed with

Why Teens Fail...

Teens and adults alike are bombarded with unfiltered noise—physiological and psychological distractions that prevent us from focusing on one problem for any length of time and inhibit our abilities to communicate about such problems.

What To Fix...

We need time each day to sit quietly and reflect on the things that are important to us, including the important relationships and necessary tasks we will encounter that day. Try to set aside designated quiet time to just think about important things.

WTF

noise and so are we! Maybe we should consider this when we research ADD/ADHD. How could our children not have attention issues and impulse control trouble with all this overstimulation? Their brains are overloaded!

Teens have less time, more to do, more noise, and more exposure to conflicting messages than in the past. Personally, it makes me feel like screaming on their behalf. As parents, we need to turn it down, filter some of this noise out of their lives; it's too much for any one human being to handle. Noise interrupts the ability to listen accurately and emanates in all sorts of forms such as hunger, emotional disruption, lighting, sounds, music, and CMC devices. It can be physiological or psychological. It's like interference on a radio station when you're listening to your favorite sports game (go, Suns!) and driving through the mountains. Sometimes you can pick up the score or play call and sometimes you can't; there is too much static.

When our listening skills are poor, it provides fabulous opportunities for making assumptions, one of the worse communication patterns to reinforce to our children. How much listening fidelity (degree of congruence between intended message sent and message received) is occurring between two family members when communicating?

Are we checking our listening and reinforcing good listening skills within our family? Feedback I receive from counselors and students indicates that parents are also busier than ever, but their teens feel as if they are being heard and not listened to. It is not our teens' fault that time is limited; we have created this chaotic lifestyle for them to try and adapt to. If it isn't easy for us, it is even more difficult for them to navigate this world. A general overview of the difference may be helpful. After all, we are not born with good listening; it is a learned skill.

Why Teens Fail...

Parents and teens alike sometimes confuse the action of "hearing" with the skill of "listening." Quality listeners practice these skills, are typically respected individuals, and develop such skills over time. Listening is not innate, but rather learned behaviors.

What To Fix...

Hearing is the physical act of processing sound and distinguishing between different notes and tones. Listening has five parts: hearing, attending, understanding, remembering, and responding.

WTF

Strategies to Succeed

Family members do not understand or distinguish the difference between listening and hearing. As parents, we need to establish a common understanding. The following is the five parts of listening according to Adler et. al. While hearing is the physiological aspect, *attending* is the psychological process where we select the key pieces of messages to focus on. Sometimes the listener focuses on aspects of the message that the sender did not emphasize. We all listen for information that matches our understanding of our world and sometimes reject anything contradictory to our beliefs. *Understanding* itself has several components which include an awareness of language, word connotation and denotation, and being informed about the source (sender) of the message and his or her personal background, culture, and experiences. Understanding also includes the mental ability to place this information all together. *Remembering* is plainly recalling the information from the pathways you've established in your brain. And lastly, *responding* involves feedback offered to the speaker. The end of the listening process is a great time for clarifications, restatements, and open-ended questioning to ensure a congruent understanding (Adler, et. al., 2012).

> **Why Teens Fail...**
>
> *Many parents have a difficult time deciding when it is appropriate to admit our own fallibilities to our children. Too often and we may seem weak; too infrequently and we may seem stubborn and hypocritical.*

> **What To Fix...**
>
> *Be prepared to admit your faults to yourself.*
>
> *Acknowledge to your teen that you know you are not perfect.*
>
> *Be your teen's parent— not their best friend! Know the difference.*

Building Self-Concepts: Building the Great Wall of China
True Parent Story: "I'm Sorry," by Kelly O.

It was early in my daughter's eighth grade year, and as usual she was huddled with a group of girls she has known since kindergarten. One of my daughter's close friends was bantering with her "boyfriend." Keep in mind that at this age you are not required to actually go out, to be going out with someone, and most relationships are negotiations by friends of friends. Her "boyfriend" wanted "an inappropriate oral sexual act." The details are a bit fuzzy about the next few events leading up to the trip to the bathroom, and I'm not sure that it is really important, but my daughter explained that not one of them really knew why it happened or had any clarity as to who thought going to the girls' restroom (one boy, one girlfriend, and two sidekicks) was a good idea. So boyfriend and girlfriend occupied the handicap stall, sidekick 1 (this would be my daughter) held the stall door and sidekick 2 was posted at the door. All were saved not by the bell but an astute teacher. Their plans were foiled long before any damage had been done to anyone's reputations. I received an afternoon call from the girlfriend's mother, even before the school had time to call. Through sobbing grief, she apologized and recounted the events as she knew them to be. Imagine, I had been the girlfriend's Girl Scout leader, and we'd had play dates for the past nine years; her mother and I had been friends for years. On my way to pick up side-kick 1 from the bus stop, I teetered among rage, humiliation, disappointment, and fear.

I rehearsed our conversation in my head again and again. There she was. Those first few moments together were tough. I allowed the silence, knowing she was uncomfortable, and I needed the moments since I was not sure exactly which of my emotions would surface first. Lips pursed and earlobes throbbing red, I began the interrogation.

Mom: What were you thinking?

Sidekick 1: (Silence)

Mom: How were you helping your friend make good choices?

Sidekick 1: (Silence)

Mom: What were you hoping to see?

The emotional wall broke and she showed her hand. The next statement would forever change the way I saw my daughter.

Sidekick 1: I was just curious.

As if lightning had struck, the epiphany happened! I knew instantly that I was the true source of the problem. My beautiful daughter was changing, maturing, and I had not equipped her with the tools to meet the challenges she was now facing. I had not acknowledged the effects her hormones played in her ability to use reason in choices, and worse, I had not empowered her to take control of her body while standing firm in her beliefs. My next statement went so far as to change the dynamics of our whole relationship.

Mom: I am so sorry. Please forgive me.

Why Teens Fail...

Parents sometimes forget that the most shocking teen behaviors are related to the most basic human needs and curiosities. As such, we sometimes make hasty judgments against a child's character rather that the behavior itself.

What To Fix...

While we should not condone attitudes or behaviors that contradict our family values, we should be cautious to never use our words to induce shame in our teens as they transition from childhood to adulthood.

She was looking for information about something so normal and so wonderful, but I had missed it. I was the one who now sat in uncomfortable silence with emotional tears. As with all parenting mistakes, you simply cannot get stuck. No child comes with a book, and for homes with multiple personalities (many children), we all struggle to be what everyone needs.

Professional Analysis

The power of words and use of words can be an impassible yield sign for parents within an interpersonal communication exchange, while the power and use of nonverbal communication is an impassible stop sign. Your teens may not know how to tell you something, but 65 percent of the time, a person's nonverbal behavior will be more accurate than their words. Then there are times when verbal and nonverbal communications contradict and we know something is amiss. Parents have to be able to juggle six bowling pins at once. I wish us all the best of luck; it will take practice! We too don't always make the best choices, and painful as it may be, we don't always have the blueprint ready for construction. I guess we have to admit, that mistakes are a part of the human condition.

We have to pay attention to verbal and nonverbal signs, practice strong listening skills, find family time and places to communicate, learn how to say "I'm sorry," know that we can *not* be our children's friends, build self-concepts, and illuminate positive self-esteem within our children. Preparing them for their next stages, we have to predict, prepare, and plan for the different growth spurts. We all know they come fast and often; it's difficult to keep up. How can we pay attention to all the signs, empower our children, and provide them with the ability to speak and act with confidence? It's like building the Great Wall of China, ensuring an inner sanctuary of beliefs and safety for your child (self-concept) while keeping negative outside influences at bay and maintaining our teens' self-esteem.

As mentioned earlier in this chapter, teens are developing their self-concept based on their set perceptions of their world, including their exposure to peer

> **Why Teens Fail...**
>
> Parents and teens are both guilty of sarcasm, the act of deliberately contradicting one's body language or tone with the verbal message. Even when done with the intent of humor, sarcasm can create mistrust and communication conflict.

> **What To Fix...**
>
> Keep sarcasm to a minimum.
>
> Offer sincere praise often.
>
> Limit criticism to important areas and attack the problem with action rather than attacking the person.

pressures, expectations at home, and expectations from their in-group and school. All these interpersonal interactions between others and your teen add up to the development of his or her self-concept. Teens will compare themselves to their relevant peer groups, using social comparisons as the basis for them to evaluate their self-worth. How do we prepare them to stand up for themselves and reaffirm strong self-concepts within their day-to-day interactions with their peers? First we have to understand the difference between self-concept and self-esteem to better equip ourselves for construction rules if we plan on building the Great Wall.

Strategies to Succeed

Did you know that the sense of self emerges in children from six to seven months of age and is influenced through their communication interactions? These communication interactions and awareness of self, form your child's self-concept. The transformation from childhood to adulthood takes place through our social comparisons of membership within our in-groups and out-groups, and our reflected appraisal of and judgments by others. Therefore our teen's self-concept evolves into a continuum of high, medium, and low self-concepts. It directly affects behaviors within their communication with others. Much like when teachers grade a writing assignment, a self-concept is subjective. Can your teens have unrealistic self-evaluations of themselves, either too positive or too negative? You can surmise the challenges and behaviors portrayed when communicating with these false perceptions and why teens may not "catch" why others' reflection of them is different than their perceived evaluation. Be realistic and honest while encouraging of your teen's strengths and weaknesses. You do not need to candy-coat their weaknesses to the point where they may perceive those weaknesses to be a strength. Ask them questions to assess their own weaknesses, and evaluate them out loud by modeling reflections of your own strengths and weaknesses. Set family and personal goals as a group, and develop thinking within the family unit.

Within the varying chapters of this book, we the authors hope to forge brain pathways, much like that of a tractor in a field, by imparting our knowledge and sharing stories. As a group of professionals, we are your network of knowledge for today's family. We are your guides, your resource center, and your toolbox, providing you with necessary tips and aid, helping you to navigate your world. After all, today it takes a knowledgeable community willing to collaborate in order to increase teen success.

Bibliography

Adler, Ronald B. et al., *Interplay: The Process of Interpersonal Communication*, (New York: Oxford University Press, 2012), 219-222.

Beebe, Steven A. and John T. Masterson, *Communicating in Small Groups: Principles and Practices*, (Boston: Allyn & Bacon, 2012), 24-25.

APPENDIX A
Brief Glossary of Texting Acronyms

BF—*Boyfriend*

BFF—*Best Friends Forever*

BFFL—*Best Friends For Life*

BTW—*By the Way*

GF—*Girlfriend*

H&K—*Hugs and Kisses*

I<3U—*I "Heart" You*

IDK—*I Don't Know*

LMAO—*Laughing My A** Off*

LMFAO—*Laughing My F****** A** Off*

LOL—*Laugh Out Loud*

OMG—*Oh My G***

ROFL—*Rolling on Floor Laughing*

WTF—*What the F***?!*

APPENDIX B
Family Data Plan Contract

1. I understand that as a minor, I am still on my parent/guardian's telephone service provider contract, and as such I have an obligation to meet my parent/guardian's expectations of behavior regarding the use of my cellular phone and/or data plan.

2. I will be responsible for the monthly payment of my data plan for the duration of the service provider contact to the extent that my parent/guardian expects me to be.

3. I will uphold our family values and represent my family with dignity while using my cell phone for communications and Internet use.

4. I will not display any personal information on my social media profiles and/or communications, including full names, dates of birth, locations of home or school, etc.

5. I will not transmit (send or receive) any media (texts, pictures, or videos) that violates our family values or any state laws.

6. If I receive any media that violates our family values or any state laws, I will report it immediately to one of the adult signers of this contract.

7. I will agree to the installation and use of any parental control software applications should my parent/guardian decide to use them.

8. I will not permit younger siblings or children to use the Internet without specific permission from my parent/guardian.

9. I will not meet anyone in person whom I only know from Internet contact without specific permission from my parent/guardian.

10. I will not use my cell phone to engage in any harassing, threatening, or otherwise illegal behavior. I understand that ignorance of the law is not an excuse.

11. I will disclose all user names and passwords for all accounts accessible by my cell phone only to my parent/guardian and no one else.

12. I understand that violation of any of the terms of this contract may result in the loss of my cell phone and data plan privileges until my parent/guardian restores such privileges, but that I will continue to be responsible for payment of my data plan as determined above (see #2).

_____   _____

Adult Parent/Guardian Signature   Date

_____   _____

Adult Parent/Guardian Signature   Date

_____   _____

Minor's Signature   Date

APPENDIX C
Family Communication Matrix

Computer Mediated Communication (CMC) used	Awareness of Communication Factors	Audience	Communication Issues/When to Use	Other Issues
Media-Rich Channels of Communication, Skype, Video Conferencing, YouTube, Cell Phone	Audio Visual	People you know personally, face to face. Family & friends from your in-group, etc.	NOISE (static, background interference, connection interruptions, etc.) impacting the quality both verbal and nonverbal messages. Use when your message is ambiguous, when your communication could be misunderstood due to messages possibly being too complicated. With cell phone, there is no verbal sight of communicator, but you do have verbal fluctuations, topic changers, pauses, etc. These other distinguishable vocal cues assign different meanings.	*All of this information can always be located in the cyber junkyard.*
Media-Lean Channels of Communication Facebook, Texting, E-mail (Beebe & Masterson, 2012)	Text and photographs with no verbal or nonverbal communication, just written words which can be subject to assumption making	People you don't know very well—professional business, committee involvement, clubs work, study groups, etc.	Uninhibited attitude by sender and receiver. Higher disclosure of personal information including photographs. Conflicts, communication when heightened emotion is involved, reactionary communication. Use this type of communication when you are describing routine content, summaries up for review, or clear and simple communication such as directions.	*Because of increased disclosure, be aware of your future. You wouldn't want future employers to see it.*

ABOUT THE AUTHORS (alphabetically listed)

Adam Brooks is an Arizona native who was a first-generation college student. Adam has a degree in speech communications as well as a master's in special education and a graduate degree in leadership development. As the instructional leader for special education at a high school in downtown Phoenix as well as a speaker at Remuda Ranch Eating Disorder/Anxiety Health Clinic, Adam has connected with youth at such a high level that he began traveling and speaking around Arizona and the United States in 2010. Since then Adam has been the keynote speaker at Arizona's SADD state conference, Thespian Leadership Camp, Jolt/4H Leadership Camp, Campference, Texas Lions Camp, and New Mexico State's student leadership retreat for 4H. He has continued to present at high schools and conferences in Arizona, New Mexico, Vermont, Texas, and Atlantic City. Adam lives in Phoenix, where he continues to teach and work on various projects that support his national speaking.

Shannon Butler has her BA degree in communication from Arizona State University, a master's in educational leadership from Northern Arizona University, and has educational certificates to teach at the K–12 and community college level. Shannon has sixteen years of service teaching middle school students in language arts and social studies and as an adjunct instructor for communication courses at the community college level. A native Minnesotan, Shannon resides in Phoenix, where she continues to educate others at all levels, parent her two lovely boys, enjoy her husband, Martin, and work on various projects that support communication and family/teen dynamics.

Tanya Corder is a police detective in the Internet Crimes Against Children Detail. This detail is currently tasked with the proactive and reactive enforcement of all Internet crimes relating to the exploitation of children. Detective Corder received her bachelor's degree in education (K–8) and later earned her master's in educational leadership from Northern Arizona University in 2006. Detective Corder has done hundreds of Internet safety presentations to help educate parents and children on the dangers that occur with the Internet, and to teach children about twenty-first century responsibilities.

Frank Griffitts has his bachelor's in applied management with an associate's degree in criminal justice. He has been a police officer/ detective since 2002. During his tenure as a police detective, he has served in the School Resource Unit (Arizona SRO of the Year, 2006), Financial Crimes Unit, and now the Computer Crimes Unit. Frank is a certified computer hard drive forensic examiner, investigating a variety of crimes including luring minors and sexual exploitation of minors. Frank is happily married to his college sweetheart, and they are currently busily engaged in raising their seven wonderful children.

John Iannarelli, with over twenty years in law enforcement, has served as a police officer with the San Diego Police Department and as a federal agent specializing in the field of cybercrime. He is also an attorney admitted to the practice of law in California, Maryland, and the District of Columbia. In 2012, Mr. Iannarelli was awarded an honorary doctorate of computer science from the University of Advancing Technology, recognizing his significant contributions to the field of combating cybercrime.

Laurie Latham is the owner and lead instructor of AZ PlayItSafe Defense, a self-defense company located in Phoenix which teaches women and children realistic strategies to stay safe from potential danger. Laurie is a former police detective with over twenty combined years of experience in both law enforcement and the security field, and is a nationally recognized security expert. She has trained thousands of police officers, women, and children in self-defense and personal protection. Laurie also has extensive knowledge in the use of personal defense products, such as pepper spray, impact weapons, and Taser. She is a certified "Girls On Guard" instructor for the Women's Self-Defense Institute and a certified protective security operator. Laurie's passion is empowering women and children and giving them the tools they need to be confident, powerful, and self-reliant. Laurie is the mother of three children and has a master's degree in educational leadership from Northern Arizona University.

Katey McPhersen is a veteran school teacher with experience in school administration as an assistant principal and a guidance counselor. She is also the founder of the SHE. Forum, the event that launched BE THE ONE. Katey was motivated to start a forum of kids and their parents when in 2004 a middle school student, bullied on the Internet, brought a knife to school and attempted to commit suicide. Now, with four daughters of her own, she strives to bring her stories and solutions to parents and teens so that they can survive and thrive in this age of social networking and digital media. While schools everywhere struggle to get the bully dilemma under control, Katey brings this message to kids and parents: BE THE ONE to create a culture of dignity!

Brooke Scritchfield has been with the Scottsdale Police Department for fourteen years. Since July of 2004 she has been assigned as a detective to the Crimes Against Persons section, where she has served in the Domestic Violence Unit and, for the past six years, in the Special Victims Unit (SVU). Detective Scritchfield has extensive knowledge of adult and child sexual assault and abuse investigations and has been case agent on and assisted with the prosecution of numerous sexual offenders. Detective Scritchfield continues to educate her department on missing and abducted children protocols. Brooke is a wife and mother of two amazing children.

Stephanie Siete is the director of public relations for Community Bridges. She is an expert prevention trainer on drug trends and resources, spending the majority of her time educating the public about the realities of drug abuse. Stephanie is dedicated to working with service providers, probation officers, the public and private health sector, and local colleges and universities, as well as local businesses. Stephanie holds degrees in health education and mass communication. She graduated from Illinois State University with dual bachelor's degrees in 1999 and became a nationally recognized certified health education specialist that same year.

Travis Webb, LMSW, received his master's degree in direct practice social work from Arizona State University, with an emphasis on children and families. He completed internships with Hamilton High School in Chandler, Arizona, in 2008 and LDS Family Services in 2009. Since then he has worked as a psychotherapist and traumatherapist for two different counseling agencies. He currently runs his private practice nights and weekends in downtown Mesa, Arizona. Travis was hired as the behavior specialist at Hartford Sylvia Encinas Elementary School in September, 2011. He has specific training and experience in working with children, adolescents, and adults struggling through crisis, abuse, neglect, and trauma. He is the creator and sole facilitator of START (Stress, Tension & Anxiety Reduction Therapy), a modality that looks at the unique stressors children are facing in a society of ever-changing expectations. He is Level II certified in trauma release exercises. Travis lives in Mesa with his wife and son.

Made in the USA
San Bernardino, CA
15 December 2012